This book is dedicated to
Msgr. Paul J. Hayes
Priest, Mentor, and Friend

"ALL GENERATIONS WILL CALL ME BLESSED"

100 Questions and Answers About the Blessed Virgin Mary

by James J. Drummey

C.R. PUBLICATIONS INC.
345 PROSPECT STREET
NORWOOD, MASSACHUSETTS 02062

C.R. Publications Inc.
345 Prospect Street
Norwood, MA 02062
www.crpublications.com

First Printing

Cover by Ariel Design
Printed in the United States of America

ISBN 0-9776099-3-6

CONTENTS

FOREWORD

On November 1st, the Feast of All Saints, my homily placed at the head of the list of saints the Virgin Mary, the humble woman of Nazareth, the immaculately conceived, sinless mother of Jesus, the Son of God. By God's privilege, Mary was taken up to Heaven, body and soul, thus crowning a human life lived full of grace and in the presence of God, with the help of the Holy Spirit.

Throughout the long centuries, people have been fascinated by and enamored of her. Everywhere basilicas and shrines were built in her honor. Great and saintly minds have created theological and mystical works in literature and music. Liturgical traditions and all forms of art, paintings, and icons, both in Eastern and Western Christianity, have paid tribute and praise to the Mother of God in all epochs and times. Mary of Nazareth is the most loved and admired saint given to us by God.

In our age of questioning and, at times, rejection of the Faith, we need a book on Mary that can help the inquiring mind to focus on the historical and theological truths about her. This book by James Drummey, *"All Generations Will Call Me Blessed,"* provides inquisitive minds with clear and correct answers on many topics concerning the place of Mary in our Catholic Faith.

With catechetical skill and thorough historical research, Mr. Drummey answers challenging questions about Mary with depth and faithfulness to the Gospel and the teachings of the Church. All need to read this book.

If ignorance of the Scriptures can mean for many Christians ignorance of Christ, likewise knowledge of the Virgin Mary can lead souls to an increased love for her and for her Son, Jesus. This knowledge of and love for our Blessed Mother will help us to imitate her life and virtues.

+Most Rev. Emilio S. Allué, SDB
Auxiliary Bishop of Boston
Feast of All Saints, 2010

PREFACE

She was a young Jewish girl married to a carpenter and living in a small village in a remote corner of the world when a heavenly visitor asked her to become the mother of the long-awaited Messiah, the "Son of the Most High." After receiving assurance from the Angel Gabriel that the birth of Jesus would not compromise her vow of virginity, Mary of Nazareth said, "May it be done to me according to your word."

Her yes to God changed the course of human history, and this humble and pious lady has become the most famous and admired woman of all time. Her portrait has appeared numerous times on the covers of prominent news magazines, her name has long been one of the most frequently chosen for baby girls, and millions of people have flocked to places where she has appeared on earth over the centuries, places often as obscure and isolated as her home village of Nazareth.

Mother of God, Mother of the Church, and Mother of all true disciples of her Son, the Blessed Virgin Mary was indeed correct when she said that "all generations will call me blessed." Still, there are many questions about this woman and her indispensable role in salvation history. This book attempts to answer those questions and to clear up any misunderstandings about our Blessed Lady.

While any opinions expressed in this book are entirely those of the author, I wish to express gratitude to those who read the manuscript and offered helpful suggestions. This includes Bishop Emilio S. Allué, SDB, who was kind enough to write the Foreword, Rev. Francisco J. Anzoategui, James R. Gontis, and Elizabeth M. Drummey. Thanks are also extended to Rev. Albert H. Stankard, whose wonderful portrait of the Virgin Mary appears on the front cover.

James J. Drummey
Feast of the Immaculate Conception, 2010

Jesus and His Mother

Chapter 1

Marian History

Q. Who was the poet who referred to the Virgin Mary as "our tainted nature's solitary boast"?

A. It was the English poet William Wordsworth (1770-1850) in Ecclesiastical Sonnet XXV, entitled *The Virgin*. The opening lines are: "Mother! whose virgin bosom was uncrost/ With the least shade of thought to sin allied;/ "Woman! above all women glorified/ Our tainted nature's solitary boast."

Q. Why do statues of Mary sometimes show her standing on a serpent?

A. It goes back to Genesis 3:15 when God told Satan, who had appeared to Eve in the form of a serpent, that "I will put enmity between you and the woman,/ and between your offspring and hers;/ He will strike at your head,/ while you strike at his heel." The Church has seen this passage as referring to Mary, whose offspring, Jesus, will destroy the works of Satan. So Mary, the Mother of the Savior, is often shown with the serpent under her feet.

Q. Where in the Old Testament can we find foreshadowings of Mary?

A. These foreshadowings are summarized in paragraph 489 of the *Catechism of the Catholic Church:*

> "Throughout the Old Covenant, the mission of many holy women *prepared* for that of Mary. At the very beginning there was Eve; despite her disobedience, she receives the promise of a posterity that will be victorious over the evil one, as well as the promise that she will be the mother of all the living [cf. *Gen* 3:15, 20]. By virtue of this promise, Sarah conceives a son in spite of her old age [cf. *Gen* 18:10-14; 21:1-2].

> "Against all human expectation God chooses those who were considered powerless and weak to show forth his faithfulness to his promises: Hannah, the mother of Samuel; Deborah; Ruth; Judith and Esther; and many other women [cf. 1 *Cor* 1:17; *1 Sam* 1]. Mary 'stands out among the poor and humble of the Lord, who confidently hope for and receive salvation from him. After a long period of waiting, the times are fulfilled in her, the exalted Daughter of Sion, and the new plan of salvation is established' " [*LG* 55].

One clear connection between Judith and the Virgin Mary was expressed by a village elder after Judith had cut off the head of the Assyrian General Holofernes:

> "Blessed are you, daughter, by the Most High God, above all the women on earth; and blessed be the LORD God, the creator of heaven and earth, who guided your blow at the head of the chief of our enemies. Your deed of hope will never be forgotten by those who tell of the might of God" (Judith 13:18-19).

The words of Uzziah the elder would be echoed centuries later by Elizabeth when she would say to the Virgin Mary, "Most blessed are you among women" (Luke 1:42). And Judith's song of thanksgiving and praise to the Lord (Judith 16:1-17) would also resonate in Mary's canticle of praise and thanksgiving known as the Magnificat (cf. Luke 1:46-55).

Q. What do we know about Mary's parents?

A. There is nothing in the Bible about them, but Tradition identifies them as Anne (sometimes Ann) and Joachim. According to certain apocryphal works, that is, books not considered to be divinely inspired, such as *The Gospel of the Nativity of Mary, Pseudo-Matthew*, and the *Protoevangelium of James*, Anne and Joachim had been married a long time without children. After praying at length for an end to her barrenness, an angel appeared to St. Anne, told her that she would conceive, and said that her child "shall be blessed by the whole world."

The veneration of Jesus' grandparents has been constant in the Church from the beginning, and Anne's feast was put on the Roman calendar in 1481. She is the patron of widows, pregnant women, childless women, and nursemaids. Joachim has also been venerated in the Eastern Church since the early days of Christianity and in the West since the sixteenth century. He is reported to have died after witnessing the Presentation of Jesus in the Temple.

Those who object to information not specifically mentioned in Scripture need to remember that the events of the New Testament were reported orally long before they were put in writing. Those who spread the Gospel by word of mouth would surely have mentioned Anne and Joachim.

It is this oral Tradition that St. Paul was referring to when he told his followers to "stand firm and hold fast to the traditions that you were taught, either by an oral statement or by a letter of ours" (2 Thessalonians 2:15). Or that John meant when he wrote that "there are also many other things that Jesus did, but if these were to be described individually, I do not think the whole world would contain the books that would be written" (John 21:25).

Q. How do we know that Mary was a teenager when the Angel Gabriel appeared to her?

A. The tradition that Mary was in her early teens when the Annunciation occurred is based on a knowledge of Jewish marriage customs. Girls at that time were usually betrothed at the age of twelve or thirteen. Men were usually betrothed between the ages of eighteen and twenty-four.

By the way, betrothal was not just a promise to marry, as it is today, but was rather a legal marriage contract. Though married, the husband and wife continued to live apart with their respective families for one year if the bride was a virgin, and one month if she was a widow. The ceremony at the end of either period of time involved welcoming the wife into the husband's home.

Q. Do we know if Mary was the only woman asked to be the Mother of Jesus, and could she have said no?

A. There is nothing in Scripture or the teaching of the Church to suggest that anyone but Mary was asked to be the Mother of Jesus. St. Paul says that "when the fullness of time had come, God sent his Son, born of a woman, born under the law, to ransom those under the law, so that we might receive adoption" (Galatians 4:4-5). The "fullness of time," said Pope John Paul II (*Mother of the Redeemer,* n. 1), "indicates the moment fixed from all eternity when the Father sent his Son 'that whoever believes in him should not perish but have eternal life' " [Jn 3:16].

In the same encyclical letter, John Paul also said that when the designated time was drawing near, "she who was from eternity destined to be his Mother already existed on earth" (n. 3). Thus, Mary was chosen to be the Mother of Jesus long before time began, and no other woman was ever considered for that divine invitation. However, God never deprived Mary of her freedom to say no, but she courageously said yes, as God knew she would.

Q. When the Angel Gabriel appeared first to Zechariah (Luke 1:5-20) and then to the Virgin Mary (Luke 1:26-38), both seemed to have the same doubts, but Zechariah was struck dumb and Mary was not. Why were they treated differently?

A. Zechariah was punished because he doubted ("How shall I know this? For I am an old man, and my wife is advanced in years.") that God could give his elderly wife a child, while Mary was unpunished because she did not doubt God, but only wanted to know the manner in which she would conceive a child since she had taken a vow of virginity ("How can this be, since I have no relations with a man?").

Zechariah expressed doubt about the possibility of a miracle, and Gabriel so understood him, while Mary did not doubt the possibility of a miracle, but was inquiring (1) about her freedom to assent to such an invitation because she was a virgin and (2) about the credentials of Gabriel to make such a stupendous offer to her – to be the Mother of God. Gabriel interpreted her query not as a doubt about the power of God, but as a legitimate and prudent question about her future motherhood.

The Archangel confirmed his credentials by explaining that the power of the Holy Spirit would overshadow Mary and allow her to become a mother without loss of her virginity. He also gave her a sign by saying that her barren kinswoman Elizabeth had conceived a child in her old age, "for nothing will be impossible for God." Mary then responded: "Behold, I am the handmaid of the Lord. May it be done to me according to your word."

Q. Do we know where Mary went to visit her kinswoman Elizabeth after the Annunciation?

A. St. Luke tells us only that "Mary set out and traveled to the hill country in haste to a town of Judah, where she entered the house of Zechariah and greeted Elizabeth" (Luke 1:39-40). Many scholars have suggested that the town in Judah was Ain Karim, which was about four days' journey from Nazareth. That Mary would undertake such a long journey after learning that Elizabeth was pregnant is evidence of her love and concern for others.

Q. How did Elizabeth know that Mary was carrying the Lord?

A. Because Scripture says that Elizabeth was "filled with the holy Spirit" (Luke 1:41).

Q. Is it true that John the Baptist was freed from Original Sin when Jesus entered the house of Elizabeth?

A. There is a tradition in the Church that John the Baptist was freed from Original Sin while in the womb of Elizabeth during the visitation of Mary. This tradition is supported by the words of the Angel Gabriel, who told Zechariah that his son's name would be John and that John "will be filled with the holy Spirit even from his mother's womb" (Luke 1:13, 15). A person still in Original Sin could not be filled with the Holy Spirit.

The Archangel's prediction came true during the Visitation when Elizabeth said, "Most blessed are you among women, and blessed is the fruit of your womb. And how does this happen to me, that the mother of my Lord should come to me? For at the moment the sound of your greeting reached my ears, the infant in my womb leaped for joy" (Luke 1:42-44).

This leaping of John in his mother's womb is thought to signify the Baptist's release from Original Sin. It is not to be confused with Mary, who was *conceived* without Original Sin.

Q. What was the manner of Jesus' birth? Did Mary experience labor pains while giving birth to Him?

A. The best analogy that we have heard is that the birth of our Lord was like a ray of sunshine passing through a window without disturbing the pane of glass. Others have compared the birth of Jesus to the coming forth of the glorified Christ from the tomb on Easter morning, or His passage through closed doors on Easter Sunday night. Referring to our Lady's title "Star of the Sea," St. Bernard wrote:

> "There is indeed a wonderful appropriateness in this comparison of her to a star because as a star sends out its ray without detriment to itself, so did the Virgin Mary bring forth her Child without injury to her integrity. And as the ray emitted does not diminish the brightness of the star, so neither did the Child born of her tarnish the beauty of Mary's virginity."

Since labor pains are associated with the consequences of Original Sin (cf. Genesis 3:16), and Mary did not have Original Sin (her Immaculate Conception), she did not suffer labor pains during the birth of Jesus.

Q. Did Mary really know that she was the Mother of God before the Resurrection of her Son?

A. Of course she did. First, she heard the words of the Angel Gabriel at the Annunciation:

> "Behold, you will conceive in your womb and bear a son, and you shall name him Jesus. He will be great and will be called Son of the Most High, and the Lord God will give him the throne of David his father, and he will rule over the house of Jacob forever, and of his kingdom there will be no end .... The holy Spirit will come upon you, and the power of the Most High will overshadow you. Therefore the child to be born will be called holy, the Son of God" (Luke 1:31-35).

Second, there are the words of Elizabeth, who told Mary, "Most blessed are you among women, and blessed is the fruit of your womb. And how does this happen to me, that the mother of my Lord should come to me?" (Luke 1:42-43).

Third, there are Mary's own words in her canticle of praise known as the Magnificat (cf. Luke 1:46-49):

> "My soul proclaims the greatness of the Lord;
> my spirit rejoices in God my savior.
> For he has looked upon his handmaid's lowliness;
> behold, from now on will all ages call me blessed.
> The Mighty One has done great things for me,
> and holy is his name."

Mary may have only been a teenager, but she was not dense or naïve. She understood what the angel was asking and even inquired how it could be in light of her vow of virginity. Satisfied with the angel's explanation, she unhesitatingly said yes to God.

If her holy offspring was to be called "Son of the Most High" and "Son of God," and if she was to be called the "mother of my Lord," and if her pregnancy had come about without the cooperation of her husband Joseph, or any other man, then Mary surely knew that something unique was happening and that this Child she was carrying was special. There was no Original Sin to cloud her mind since she had been conceived immaculate in her mother's womb, so Mary was not ignorant about the divinity of her Son.

Q. Why did Mary need to present herself in the Temple for purification if she was "full of grace"?

A. It is true that Mary had no need of being purified since she was free from all sin from the moment of her conception in her mother's womb. But she came to the Temple for purification because it was required by the Mosaic law, and she was always obedient to the law. According to Leviticus 12:2-8, a woman who gave birth to a boy was to come to the Temple forty days after the birth and offer a year-old lamb as a burnt offering and a turtledove or two young pigeons as an expiation for sin. A woman who could not afford a lamb could offer instead two turtledoves or two young pigeons, as Mary did, in order to fulfill "all the prescriptions of the law of the Lord" (Luke 2:39).

Q. Can we reconcile the timing of the Presentation of Jesus in the Temple with the flight of the Holy Family into Egypt? How long did they stay in Egypt?

A. Unlike modern-day historians, the Evangelists were not concerned with the precise chronological sequence of events, and one has to look at both Matthew and Luke to piece together the Infancy narrative. According to the Mosaic law, a woman who had delivered a male child was to present herself in the Temple for purification forty days after the birth and also to consecrate a first-born son to the Lord, and then redeem him for five shekels.

Thus, Mary and Joseph traveled to Jerusalem forty days after the birth of Christ and fulfilled both prescriptions of the law. They then returned to Bethlehem and were living in a house when the Magi arrived. So the Presentation took place before the arrival of the Wise Men and the flight into Egypt.

The Magi had been asked by King Herod to let him know

the location of the newborn king of the Jews so that he could go and pay Him homage (in reality to kill Him). But they were warned in a dream of Herod's evil intentions and returned home by another route. The same angelic warning was given to Joseph in a dream, and he quickly set out for Egypt with Mary and the Christ Child.

The Holy Family remained in Egypt until word came of Herod's death, and the refugees returned to their own country, eventually settling in Nazareth. The Gospels do not give us the exact duration of their sojourn in Egypt, but reliable historians, such as Giuseppe Ricciotti (cf. *The Life of Christ,* pp. 257-259), estimate that their stay may have been only a few months.

Q. I have heard it said that Jesus, Mary, and Joseph were just an "ordinary Jewish family" prior to the public ministry of Jesus. Is that true? How could they be just an ordinary Jewish family in light of Mary's Immaculate Conception, her perpetual virginity, and Joseph's chastity?

A. We know virtually nothing about the first thirty years of Jesus' life, except for the circumstances surrounding His birth and the time when He was lost in the Temple in Jerusalem at the age of twelve. Knowing something about life in first-century Palestine, however, we can surmise what growing up was like for our Lord. While the special privileges granted to Mary and Joseph were anything but ordinary, those privileges would not have been known to their friends and neighbors in Nazareth. They would have seen the Holy Family as an ordinary Jewish family. Here is how Giuseppe Ricciotti summarizes the hidden years of Jesus in his *Life of Christ,* pp. 265-266:

> "Big things had been happening around the world in those thirty years .... In Nazareth, meanwhile, it was as though Jesus did not exist. Similar outwardly to all those of his own age, he danced on his mother's knee, then helped her child-fashion, then assisted Joseph in the shop, later began to read and write, recited the … customary prayers, attended the synagogue. As

a young man, he probably took an interest in the fields and the vineyards, in the work Joseph was doing ... in questions concerning the Jewish Law, in the Pharisees and Sadducees, in the political events in Palestine and abroad. To all appearances his days were spent quite simply in this wise.

"His daily language was Aramaic, spoken with an accent peculiar to the Galileans, which betrayed them the minute they began to talk. But since his country was a border territory in which there was continual contact with the surrounding Greek populations, a certain knowledge of Greek was almost necessary. Hence it is probable that he used Greek sometimes and even more probable that he used Hebrew.

"Jesus also had relatives .... Those who are closest are designated by the term 'brothers' and 'sisters,' though they may be only cousins of various degree. In the Hebrew Bible the nouns *ah*, 'brother,' and *ahoth*, 'sister' often denote persons far removed in kinship, especially since in ancient Hebrew there is no precise term for cousin exclusively. The 'brothers' and 'sisters' of Jesus, therefore, were his cousins.

"Now, not all of these many relatives looked on Jesus with favor. In the middle of his public life we find that 'not even his brethren believed in him' (John 7:5). Nor is it reasonable to suppose that this antipathy began with Jesus' public life. It must have been rather the open manifestation of an old feeling toward him which had brooded in the hearts of his kinsmen even during his life in Nazareth. Jesus himself gives us the reason for this, though in general terms: 'A prophet is not without honor except in his own country, and among his own kindred, and in his own house' (Mark 6:4).

"In any case, besides these resentful kinsmen, there were others most faithful to him ... who undoubtedly surrounded him with their kindness even while he was still an obscure boy and youth in Nazareth. First among them all were Mary and Joseph, then 'James the brother of the Lord' (Gal. 1:19) ... then others (Acts 1:14), some of whom perhaps had shed with time their earlier resentment."

Q. What are the seven sorrows of the Virgin Mary?

A. Also known as the Seven Dolors of the Blessed Mother, they are the prophecy of Simeon that Mary's heart would be pierced by a sword (Luke 2:34-35), the flight into Egypt to escape the murderous wrath of King Herod (Matthew 2:13-23), the three-day separation from Jesus in Jerusalem when He was twelve years old (Luke 2:41-50), the meeting with her Son on the road to Calvary, the Crucifixion and Death of our Lord, the placing of His body in Mary's arms after it was taken down from the Cross, and His burial in the tomb provided by Joseph of Arimathea.

The feast of Our Lady of Sorrows is celebrated on September 15th.

Q. What did Simeon mean in Luke 2:34-35 when he said to Mary that "this child is destined for the fall and rise of many in Israel, and to be a sign that will be contradicted (and you yourself a sword will pierce) so that the thoughts of many hearts may be revealed"?

A. This means that Mary would also suffer along with her Son not only on the road to Calvary and at the foot of the Cross, but also when He and His teachings provoked animosity and hatred among His listeners as people chose sides and showed by words and actions the thoughts contained within their hearts. Jesus was able to read those hostile hearts and to know what His enemies were thinking and planning.

Simeon was predicting that spiritual downfall would come to those who rejected Jesus, while those who chose to follow Him would rise spiritually in the sight of God. He was also predicting the Seven Sorrows of Mary.

Q. We know that pain and suffering came into the world because of Original Sin. But Mary did not have Original Sin, so how do we explain her sufferings?

A. By recognizing that Mary was wholly united with her Son from the moment of the Incarnation until His death on the Cross and wanted to share in all the events of His life, events that we recall in the Joyful, Luminous, Sorrowful, and Glorious Mysteries of the rosary. She more than any other person was willing to take up her cross every day and faithfully follow Jesus out of love for the Father and for the sake of her spiritual children in the world.

Thus, said the Second Vatican Council in its *Dogmatic Constitution on the Church* (n. 58), "the Blessed Virgin advanced in her pilgrimage of faith, and loyally persevered in her union with her Son unto the cross. There she stood, in keeping with the divine plan (cf. John 19:25), suffering grievously with her only-begotten Son. There she united herself with a maternal heart to His sacrifice, and lovingly consented to the immolation of this Victim, which she herself had brought forth. Finally, the same Christ Jesus dying on the cross gave her as a mother to His disciple. This He did when He said: 'Woman, behold thy Son' (cf. John 19:26-27)."

Q. What evidence is there that Mary lived in Ephesus (modern-day Turkey) near the end of her life on earth?

A. Tradition tells us that John the Apostle lived for a time in Ephesus and eventually died there. For example, St. Irenaeus (140-202) said in *Against Heresies* that John wrote the fourth Gospel "while he was residing at Ephesus in Asia." And St. Polycrates of Ephesus (125-196), in a letter to Pope St. Victor around A.D. 190, said that the same John who reclined at the bosom of the Lord at the Last Supper "fell asleep at Ephesus."

Since Jesus on the Cross entrusted the care of His mother to John (cf. John 19:26-27), it is believed that the Blessed Virgin spent some time with the evangelist in Ephesus before the end of her life. There is a dwelling in that city that has been venerated since ancient times as the place where the Blessed Mother lived. Thousands of pilgrims visit the house every year, and several recent Popes have prayed there.

For more information about this holy site, see pages 177-178 of Joan Carroll Cruz's book *Relics*. According to Mrs. Cruz, "the little house is called Panaya Kapulu, the house of the Holy Virgin. It has become the object of so many pilgrimages that the Turkish authorities have built an excellent road to its entrance. It is estimated by one authority that 10,000 people of all faiths visit the shrine each week."

Q. What about the tradition that the house of Mary in Nazareth was miraculously transported by angels to Italy in the thirteenth century?

A. In 1852, Blessed Pope Pius IX wrote in the bull *Inter Omnia:* "Venerated in Loreto is that House of Nazareth, so loved by the Heart of God, and that, built in Galilee, was later separated from its foundation and, by divine power, translated beyond the sea, first to Dalmatia and then to Italy." The tradition holds that the house was miraculously transported from Nazareth to Tersatto (in present-day Croatia) in 1291 and then to Loreto in Italy.

Although there are those who are skeptical about this tradition, it received support in 2006, when a study concluded that the stones in the Grotto of the Annunciation in Nazareth have the same origin as the stones in an altar at the Holy House of Loreto. Giorgio Nicolini, author of a book on the Holy House, said that "there was never any doubt" about the authenticity of the house "other than on the part of those who are not acquainted with the secular studies in this respect. So much so that, for seven centuries, all the Sovereign Pontiffs confirmed the authenticity with solemn canonical acts of 'approval.' "

The new study regarding the Altar of the Apostles in the house, said Nicolini, "is important because, in addition to providing a further proof of the authenticity of the Holy House of Loreto as Mary's Nazarene House, it also provides an even more spectacular proof in regard to the miraculousness of the translation of the Holy House of Nazareth."

The Holy House is a small stone building measuring 13 by

31 feet that has, since 1469, been enclosed by a large basilica. The shrine attracts as many as four million visitors each year.

Q. Did the Second Vatican Council downplay the role of the Virgin Mary?

A. No, it did not. Not only did Vatican II (1962-1965) open on the feast of the Maternity of Mary, close on the feast of the Immaculate Conception, and entrust its sessions to her protection, the Council also devoted an entire chapter to the Blessed Virgin in its Dogmatic Constitution on the Church *(Lumen Gentium)*. The document clearly encouraged Catholics to turn to Mary:

> "Let the entire body of the faithful pour forth persevering prayer to the Mother of God and Mother of men. Let them implore that she who aided the beginnings of the Church by her prayers may now, exalted as she is in heaven above all the saints and angels, intercede with her Son in the fellowship of all the saints. May she do so until all the peoples of the human family, whether they are honored with the name of Christian or whether they still do not know their Savior, are happily gathered together in peace and harmony into the one People of God, for the glory of the Most Holy and Undivided Trinity" (n. 69).

When Pope Paul VI promulgated *Lumen Gentium* in 1964, he proclaimed Mary the Mother of the Church, saying that "knowledge of the exact doctrine of the Church on Mary will always be the key to a precise understanding of the mystery of Christ and his Church. For the glory of the Virgin Mary, and for our own consolation, we proclaim Mary Mother of the Church, i.e., of the whole People of God, of the faithful as well as of the pastors. And we wish that through this title the Mother of God should be still more honored and invoked by the entire Christian people."

Q. What are some reasons that we should turn to Mary?

A. Of the many good reasons for turning to Mary, here are four: (1) She is unique among all the women of history in that she was conceived without Original Sin, gave birth to a Child without losing her virginity, and was taken up, body and soul, into Heaven at the end of her life. (2) She was given the greatest of all relationships to Jesus – the relationship of mother to son. (3) She has demonstrated her deep love and concern for us by numerous appearances on earth, especially in recent centuries. (4) Devotion to Mary helps us to be holy by imitating her virtues. She intercedes for us better than any other saint or any angel.

Q. Why do we celebrate Mary during the months of May and October?

A. May was chosen as the month of Mary during the Middle Ages to counteract pagan festivals that were common at that time of year. King Alphonsus X of Spain (died in 1284) appears to have been the first person to link Mary with the month of May, and the idea gained popularity over the next few centuries.

The practice spread rapidly in the 18th century due to the publication of several handbooks or manuals, such as *The Month of Mary*, or *The Month of May* in 1725, *The Month of Mary* in 1758, and *The Month of May* in 1785, with chapters on the life of the Blessed Mother, her virtues and privileges, and suggestions for decorating her altar or statue, reciting the rosary, and singing her litany.

By the 19th century, May was celebrated as Mary's month throughout Europe and the United States, and Popes Pius VII and Pius IX attached indulgences to the May devotions. Twentieth-century Popes also spoke favorably of Marian piety during the month of May, notably Pius XII in *Mediator Dei* (1947) and Paul VI in *Mense Maio* (1965). In the latter document, Pope Paul said:

> "It is precisely because the month of May is a powerful incentive to more fervent and trusting prayer, and because during it our petitions find their way more easily to the compassionate heart of Our Blessed Lady, that it has been a custom dear to our predecessors to choose this month,

dedicated to Mary, for inviting the Christian people to offer up public prayers, whenever the needs of the Church demanded it, or whenever danger hovered menacingly over the world."

While the origins of October as the month dedicated to our Lady and her rosary go back to the Dominican rosary devotions commemorating the victory over Turkish Muslims at Lepanto in October 1571, and to the institution of the Feast of the Holy Rosary on October 7, 1573, by Pope Gregory XIII, it was Pope Leo XIII who was particularly responsible for designating this month as one devoted to the Blessed Virgin.

He ordered all parish churches to celebrate October as our Lady's month in 1883 and, in 1894, said in one of his many rosary messages that "it is always with joyful expectation and renewed hope that we look forward to the return of the month of October. At our exhortation and by our express order, this month has been consecrated to the Blessed Virgin" *(Iucunda Semper)*.

Q. Why was January 1st changed from the Feast of the Circumcision of Jesus to the Solemnity of Mary?

A. Since at least the sixth century, the Church had commemorated January 1st, the Octave of Christmas, as the Circumcision of Our Lord. The feast recalled the initiation of Jesus into Judaism (cf. Luke 2:21) and foreshadowed our initiation into the Church through the Sacrament of Baptism. In 1970, the Church decided to reemphasize Mary's role in the Incarnation by changing the name of the feast to the Solemnity of Mary, Mother of God. This holy day of obligation takes the place of the former feast of the Maternity of Mary, which was observed on October 11th.

Q. Why are altars and statues of the Blessed Virgin Mary on the left side of the main altar?

A. According to J.B. O'Connell's book *Church Building and Furnishing: The Church's Way* (p. 165), "the more dignified side altars are placed nearer the high altar (the most dignified on the Gospel side)." Another commentator says that "the longstanding custom of placing our Lady's statue to the left side of the sanctuary is derived from the very old iconographic convention of placing her image to the left of the painted, carved, or sculpted crucifix in the sanctuary. The iconographic convention has two meanings. The first meaning comes from Psalm 45 as applied to our Lady in the liturgy: 'The queen takes her place at your right hand....' Thus, Mary is depicted standing at the right hand of Christ, that is to say, to the viewer's left.

> "The second meaning is that from very early times the figure of our Lady to the left of the crucifix symbolized the Old Testament and life on this earth, while the figure of St. John on the right side symbolized the New Testament and the life to come. As for the church sanctuary itself, it faced east, the direction which symbolized the Second Coming of Christ: 'As the lightning from the east flashes to the west, so will the coming of the Son of Man be' (Matthew 24:27).
>
> "But even more importantly, the direction east alludes to the direction the Temple high priest faced when offering sacrifice. Because Christ is called the Temple high priest in the book of Hebrews, He was always seen as facing east when offering the Sacrifice of the Mass to the Father through the actions of the earthly priest."

Q. What do you know about Archbishop Fulton Sheen's statement that the Virgin Mary would play a key role in the conversion of Muslims to Christianity?

A. In his book *The World's First Love*, Fulton Sheen pointed out that the Koran, which is the bible of Islam, contains many passages about Mary and affirms belief in her Immaculate Conception and the Virgin Birth. He said that Muslims hold Mary in high esteem, and she is rivaled only by Fatima, the daughter of Mohammed.

Sheen noted that when the Muslims were finally driven out of Portugal, the last Muslim chief had a daughter named Fatima, who fell in love with a Catholic man. She not only stayed behind when her people left, but she became a Catholic. Her husband was so much in love with her that he changed the name of the town where they lived to Fatima. "Thus," said Archbishop Sheen, "the very place where Our Lady appeared in 1917 bears a historical connection to Fatima, the daughter of Mohammed."

It was no coincidence, said Sheen, that "the Blessed Mother, in the 20th century, should have revealed herself in the significant little village of Fatima, so that to all future generations she would be known as Our Lady of Fatima. Since nothing ever happens out of Heaven except with a finesse of all the details, I believe that the Blessed Virgin chose to be known as Our Lady of Fatima as a pledge and a sign of hope to the Muslim people, and as an assurance that they, who show her so much respect, will one day accept her divine Son, too."

The Archbishop said back in 1952 that missionaries to the Muslim world "will be successful in the measure that they preach Our Lady of Fatima. Mary is the advent of Christ, bringing Christ to the people before Christ Himself is born. In an apologetic endeavor, it is always best to start with that which people already accept. Because the Muslims have a devotion to Mary, our missionaries should be satisfied merely to expand and to develop that devotion, with the full realization that Our Blessed Lady will carry the Muslims the rest of the way to her divine Son."

Sheen said that Mary is "forever a traitor, in the sense that she will not accept any devotion for herself, but will always bring anyone who is devoted to her to her divine Son. As those who lose devotion to her lose belief in the divinity of Christ, so those who intensify devotion to her gradually acquire that belief."

Chapter 2

Marian Misunderstandings

Q. Do Catholics adore the Virgin Mary and make her equal to Jesus?

A. No, Catholics only adore God, but they do pay high honor to Mary for the holy life she led and because she was chosen by God to be the mother of His Son. The Fourth Commandment tells us to honor mothers and fathers. Did Jesus keep this commandment by honoring His mother? Of course He did. So in honoring Mary we are just following the example of our Lord. What's wrong with honoring the holiest woman who ever lived? We are like the "beloved disciple" who took Mary "into his home" (John 19:27).

The Bible tells us to call Mary "blessed" (Luke 1:48), so Catholics are just following Scripture when they pay tribute to the Blessed Mother. Does this tribute take away from our worship of Jesus? Not at all. Devotion to Mary always leads us to her Son. Mary's final words in the Gospels, speaking about her Son at the wedding feast in Cana, suggest the course that we are to follow: "Do whatever he tells you" (John 2:5).

Q. What about those who want to have Mary declared co-redeemer with Jesus?

A. Catholics believe that Jesus is the one Mediator between God and us and the sole Redeemer of humanity, but that His mother has been given a share in the saving role of her Son. Thus, the Virgin Mary is invoked by the Church, said the Second Vatican Council, "under the titles Advocate, Auxiliatrix, Adjutrix, and Mediatrix. These, however, are to be so understood that they neither take away from nor add anything to the dignity and efficacy of Christ the one Mediator. For no creature could ever be classed with the Incarnate Word and Redeemer" (*Lumen Gentium*, n. 62).

The Council said that "the Church does not hesitate to profess this subordinate role of Mary. She experiences it continuously and commends it to the hearts of the faithful, so that encouraged by this maternal help they may more closely adhere to the Mediator and Redeemer" (*Ibid.*).

For a correct understanding of the Virgin Mary's unique place in the Church, read the eighth chapter of *Lumen Gentium*, Pope John Paul II's encyclical letter *Mother of the Redeemer*, and paragraphs 963-975 of the *Catechism of the Catholic Church*.

Q. How can Mary, a human being, be called the Mother of God, a divine Being?

A. When a mother gives birth, she gives birth to a person, not to a nature. So the Child growing in Mary's womb for nine months was fully human, but was not only human. The Second Person of the Blessed Trinity was also divine, having always possessed a divine nature. He received His human nature from His mother, who supplied all the genetic matter for His human body. She was not just the mother of His human nature, however, but the mother of Himself. If Mary is the mother of Jesus, and Jesus is God, then Mary is the Mother of God.

When a heretic named Nestorius denied the real union of the divine and human natures of Christ and taught that, while Mary could be called the Mother of Christ as man, she could not be called the Mother of God, the Council of Ephesus declared in 431:

> "We confess, then, our Lord Jesus Christ, the only begotten Son of God, perfect God and perfect man, of a rational soul and a body, begotten before all ages from the Father in His Godhead, the same in the last days for us and for our salvation, born of Mary the Virgin according to His humanity, one and the same consubstantial with

the Father in Godhead and consubstantial with us in humanity, for a union of two natures took place.

"Therefore, we confess one Christ, one Son, one Lord. According to this understanding of the unconfused union, we confess the holy Virgin to be the Mother of God because God the Word took flesh and became man and from His very conception united to Himself the temple He took from her."

Q. What do we mean by the Immaculate Conception of the Virgin Mary?

A. The Immaculate Conception *does not* refer to the virginal conception of Jesus in Mary's womb through the power of the Holy Spirit. That is the doctrine of Mary's divine maternity. What the Immaculate Conception *does mean* is that Mary, from the first instant of her conception in the womb of her mother, St. Anne, was preserved from all stain of Original Sin. This doctrine is implied in the greeting of the Angel Gabriel to the young Jewish girl: "Hail, full of grace, the Lord is with thee" (Luke 1:28).

If Mary was full of grace at the time of the angel's visit, then she was entirely full of God's divine life and completely free from sin, including Original Sin. Jesus gave her this special privilege because He wanted to be born of a pure and sinless mother. While the Church has always taught this doctrine, it was not until 1854 that Blessed Pope Pius IX infallibly proclaimed it a dogma of the Church. Here are the words of the Holy Father:

"The Most Blessed Virgin Mary was, from the first moment of her conception, by a singular grace and privilege of Almighty God and by virtue of the merits of Jesus Christ, Savior of the human race, preserved immune from all stain of Original Sin."

It is interesting to note that, when the Blessed Virgin appeared to St. Bernadette at Lourdes in France in 1858, just four years after Pius IX's proclamation, she told the young girl, "I am the Immaculate Conception." This gave credence to Bernadette's claim to have seen our Lady because an unschooled teenage girl could not possibly have known that title of the Blessed Mother.

It is also the teaching of the Church, as reiterated in the *Catechism* (n. 493), that by the grace of God Mary remained free of every personal sin during her entire life.

Q. But didn't Mary, in her canticle of praise known as the Magnificat, call God "my Savior," implying that she was not sinless if she needed a Savior?

A. As a descendant of Adam, the Blessed Mother also required a savior since she could have contracted Original Sin at the moment her life in the womb began, but God preserved her from this plague of the human race and from all its consequences. She was redeemed by the Blood of Christ, not through Baptism but by anticipation.

The Church has for centuries explained this doctrine of "preservative redemption," which was introduced into the Church by John Duns Scotus (1266-1308), with the analogy of a deep hole with the words "Original Sin" on the muddy bottom. All members of the human race, except Mary, fall into that pit and are stained with Original Sin. The only way they can be rescued or "saved" from the pit is through the sacrament of Baptism.

Mary, on the other hand, was prevented from even falling into the hole. Jesus applied His grace to her before she could topple into the pit and be marred with Original Sin.

Q. Didn't St. Thomas Aquinas, one of the premier theologians in the history of the Church, oppose the doctrine of the Immaculate Conception?

A. Aquinas (1225-1274), along with such other devotees of the Virgin Mary as Saints Albert the Great, Bernard of Clairvaux, and Bonaventure, had trouble accepting this dogma as a revealed truth of the Faith because the doctrine "seemed to exempt Mary from being redeemed by her Son." The theological breakthrough came about when Duns Scotus explained that "some have been raised up after they have fallen, but the Virgin Mary was sustained as it were in the very act of falling, like the two men who were about to tumble into a pit."

In his classic work *Fundamentals of Catholic Dogma*, Ludwig Ott explained Mary's "pre-redemption" in these words:

> "By reason of her natural origin, she, like all other children of Adam, was subject to the necessity of contracting Original Sin, but by a special intervention of God was preserved from stain of Original Sin. Thus Mary also was redeemed 'by the grace of Christ,' but in a more perfect manner than other human beings.
>
> "While these are freed from Original Sin present in their souls, Mary, the Mother of the Redeemer, was preserved from the contagion of Original Sin. Thus the dogma of the Immaculate Conception of Mary in no way contradicts the dogma that all children of Adam are subject to Original Sin and need redemption" (p. 199).

Q. But how can Mary be called sinless when the Bible says that "all have sinned" (Romans 3:23)?

A. It was St. Paul who said that "all have sinned and are deprived of the glory of God" (Romans 3:23). In his book *Catholicism and Fundamentalism* (cf. pp. 270-271), Karl

Keating said that Fundamentalists think this verse "means Mary must have sinned during her life, and that certainly would speak against an Immaculate Conception. Is the fundamentalists' analysis solid? Not really.

> "Think about a child below the age of reason. By definition he cannot sin, since sinning requires the ability to reason and the ability to intend to sin. If the child dies before ever committing an actual sin, because he is not mature enough to know what he is doing, what act of his brings him under their interpretation of Romans 3:23? None, of course."

Keating said that Paul's comment might refer "not to absolutely everyone, but just to the mass of mankind (which means young children and other special cases, such as Mary, would be excluded without having to be singled out). If not that, then it would mean that everyone, without exception, is subject to Original Sin, which is true for a young child, for the unborn, even for Mary – but she, although due to be subject to it, was preserved from its stain."

In other words, said Keating, God acted in a positive way to preserve Mary from Original Sin in the first place. He said that "Mary received a very special kind of 'baptism' at her conception, but since she never contracted Original Sin, she enjoyed certain privileges we never can, such as entire avoidance of sin" throughout her life.

Q. The Gospels say that Jesus had "brothers" and "sisters," so how could Mary be called "ever-virgin"?

A. In Hebrew and Aramaic, the languages spoken by Jesus and His followers, there was no specific word for "cousin," so the word "brother" was used for brother, cousin, or other relatives. But we know, for example, that the James and Joseph mentioned in Matthew 13:55 as the brothers of Jesus were in fact the sons of another Mary, the wife of Clopas (cf.

Matthew 27:56). Since the Gospels also tell us that Mary of Clopas was the Blessed Virgin's "sister" (John 19:25), that means that she was Jesus' aunt and her children were His cousins.

It was not uncommon in those days, or in our own time either, to call close friends or relatives "brothers" or "sisters," as Jesus did in John 20:17, when He told Mary Magdalene to "go to my brothers and tell them, 'I am going to my Father and your Father, to my God and your God.' " But Magdalene went not to any blood brothers of Jesus, but "to the disciples" (John 20:18). Or as Peter did in Acts 1:16, when he addressed the 120 disciples gathered in the Upper Room as "my brothers."

Furthermore, if our Lord had blood brothers, wouldn't He on the Cross have entrusted His mother to their care rather than to the Apostle John (cf. John 19:26-27)?

Search the Scriptures as diligently as you can, and you will not find Mary identified as the mother of anyone but Jesus. Her perpetual virginity has been taught by the Church from the beginning and has been reaffirmed in the *Catechism* (cf. nn. 499-501). Our belief today is the same as it was in the fifth century, when St. Augustine described the Blessed Mother as "a virgin who conceives, a virgin who gives birth, a virgin with child, a virgin delivered of child – a virgin ever virgin."

Q. But what about Luke's statement (2:7) that Mary gave birth to her "firstborn son"? Or Matthew's statement (1:25) that Joseph "had no relations with her until she bore a son"?

A. That Jesus was Mary's "firstborn" son means only that He was her first child, the child who opened the womb and belonged to God (cf. Exodus 13:2, 34:20). It does not mean that there were other children later on. This firstborn son had to be taken to the Temple and consecrated to the Lord by offering a sacrifice of either a pair of turtledoves or two young pigeons (cf. Luke 2:24).

As for the statement from Matthew, the problem is that we interpret the word "until" to mean that something happened after that. But in the Bible "until" (or "till") meant only that something had not happened up to that point in time. It did not imply, as it does today, that some action did happen later. The Greek word for "until" is *heos*, which always refers to the past and never to the future.

Consider an example from the Old Testament that shows how absurd this interpretation can be if the modern sense is applied to the Bible. In 2 Samuel 6:23, it says that "Saul's daughter Michal was childless to [till] the day of her death." Does this mean that she had children *after* her death? Of course not.

In Luke 2:36-37, it says that the prophetess Anna had "lived seven years with her husband after her marriage, and then as a widow until she was eighty-four." This certainly doesn't imply that Anna got married again after the age of eighty-four. Nor does Luke 1:80, which says that John the Baptist "was in the desert until the day of his manifestation to Israel," imply that John never returned to the desert.

Q. What of the contention that St. Joseph was a widower with several children prior to marrying the Blessed Virgin Mary? Could these children have been the "brothers" and "sisters" of Jesus?

A. While the *Protoevangelium of James,* an extra-biblical book probably written in the second century, makes Joseph out to be a widower with children from a previous marriage when he married Mary, there is nothing in the canonical books of the Bible to support this theory. Some who advance this possibility may be trying to account for Joseph's willingness to enter into a celibate marriage, but Pope John Paul II shed a different light on Mary and Joseph's consecrated virginity at an audience in 1996:

> "It may be presumed that at the time of their betrothal there was an understanding between Joseph and Mary about her plan to live as a virgin. Moreover, the Holy Spirit, who had inspired Mary to choose virginity in view of the mystery of the Incarnation and who wanted the latter to come about in a family setting suited to the Child's growth, was quite able to instill in Joseph the ideal of virginity as well."

Also rejecting this theory in his book *To Know Christ Jesus* (pp. 71-72) was Frank Sheed, who said that "such an arrangement, with Joseph merely brought in to keep the neighbors from talking, would hardly be a marriage at all, but rather a mockery of marriage .... We must think of them as truly husband and wife, with a true union of personalities, each bringing completion to the other, with a profound sharing of interests, sharing of lives, enriched by the special graces from God that their virginity called for....

> "Both loved God supremely, and their love of God poured back in a great flood of love of each other, love so great that it made the ordinary outward manifestation unnecessary. There was more love in that virginal family, more married love, than ever a family has known."

Q. Isn't it true that the founders of Protestantism in the 16th century asserted the Catholic view that Mary was a virgin all her life?

A. Yes, it is true, and Protestants who assert otherwise ought to listen to their founders. For example, Martin Luther said that "Christ our Savior was the real and natural fruit of Mary's virginal womb .... This was without the cooperation of a man, and she remained a virgin after that" (*Luther's Works*, edited by Jaroslav Pelikan, vol. 22, p. 23).

In criticizing the fourth-century heretic Helvidius, John Calvin said that "Helvidius has shown himself too ignorant in saying that Mary had several sons because mention is made in some passages of the brothers of Christ." And Ulrich Zwingli, the Swiss Reformation leader, wrote: "I firmly believe according to the words of the Gospel that a pure virgin brought forth for us the Son of God and remained a virgin pure and intact in childbirth and also after the birth, for all eternity."

The Calvin and Zwingli statements can be found in the article "Protestants and Our Lady," which appeared in the January/February 1967 issue of *Marian Library Studies,* nn. 128/129.

Q. Do we know what happened to St. Joseph or when he died?

A. No, there are no records indicating when St. Joseph died or what happened to him after he is mentioned at the time Jesus was found in the Temple at the age of twelve. There is no reference to him after Jesus began His public life at the age of thirty, so the presumption is that he died sometime during those eighteen years. Joseph is considered the patron of a happy death since he presumably died in the presence of Jesus and Mary. For some wonderful insights into this good and holy man, see Pope John Paul II's apostolic exhortation *Guardian of the Redeemer.*

Q. Isn't there a story about St. Joseph building a staircase in a chapel in Santa Fe, New Mexico?

A. Yes, and the story was recounted in a 1998 CBS television movie entitled *The Staircase*. According to the story, the Loreto Chapel in Santa Fe was originally built without a way to reach the choir loft. Adding a regular staircase would have taken up too much room in the chapel, so the

Loreto nuns began a nine-day novena to St. Joseph for a solution to their dilemma.

On the final day of the novena, an elderly man arrived at the chapel on a donkey and said that he had been sent to build the staircase. Using only a hammer, a T-square, a saw, and some hot water to bend the wood, he completed the work in about eight months during the year 1878. The spiral stairway is an engineering marvel that was built without nails or any visible supports.

When the sisters went to pay the man, he had disappeared. They thought that they should at least pay for the lumber, but the only lumber yard in town had not sold any lumber to the mysterious carpenter, and the wood he had used was not found anywhere in New Mexico.

The sisters believed that St. Joseph had built the stairway, and some of the details have a religious significance. The 33 curving steps symbolize the years Jesus lived on earth, and the seven-foot diameter of the staircase and the seven-inch height of the steps signify the seven Sacraments.

A handrail and some metal braces were added decades later, and the Chapel operates today as a museum that is visited by more than 100,000 people each year. Tourists are not allowed to touch or climb the staircase, but just seeing it up close is a moving experience.

Q. It seems that there is confusion about whether or not Mary was an unwed mother. Can you clarify this?

A. The allegation that Mary was an unwed mother is false and can be refuted by carefully reading Matthew's Gospel, particularly where he says that when "Mary was betrothed to Joseph, but before they lived together, she was found with child through the holy Spirit. Joseph her husband, since he was a righteous man, yet unwilling to expose her to shame, decided to divorce her quietly" (1:18-19).

Notice that Matthew calls Joseph Mary's "husband" and says that Joseph had decided to "divorce her quietly" when he discovered that she was with child upon her return from a three-month visit to her relative Elizabeth. But how could Joseph divorce Mary unless they were already married?

Furthermore, when the angel of the Lord appeared to Joseph in a dream, he told him, "Do not be afraid to take Mary your wife into your home. For it is through the holy Spirit that this child has been conceived in her" (Matthew 1:20). The angel calls Mary Joseph's "wife."

If these plain words are not enough to convince someone that Mary and Joseph were married when Jesus was conceived, then one can explain that, according to Jewish tradition, betrothal was the ceremony that united the couple in marriage. The second stage came a year later, if the woman was a virgin, when she moved into the house of her husband. In his apostolic exhortation *Guardian of the Redeemer,* Pope John Paul II confirmed this tradition:

> "According to Jewish custom, marriage took place in two stages: first, the legal or true marriage was celebrated, and then, only after a certain period of time, the husband brought the wife into his own house. Thus, before he lived with Mary, Joseph was already her 'husband.' Mary, however, preserved her deep desire to give herself exclusively to God" (n. 18).

Q. Why at the wedding feast in Cana and at the Cross did Jesus call Mary "woman" instead of "Mother"?

A. While this might sound disrespectful to us today, it was a common and rather formal way of speaking at the time of Jesus. But it was also our Lord's way of connecting His mother with the "woman" mentioned in Genesis 3:15, who would be the enemy of Satan and whose offspring would bring about a final victory over Satan, sin, and death.

The Church has always seen Mary as that woman, the "New Eve" whose obedience would, in the words of St. Irenaeus, "untie the knot of Eve's disobedience," and Jesus as her offspring, who would be the "New Adam" by "becoming obedient to death,/ even death on a cross" (Philippians 2:8).

Q. At the Cross, Jesus mentioned Mary as John's mother, so why do we call her our mother?

A. The teaching that Mary is our mother is based on Jesus' words from the Cross: "When Jesus saw his mother and the disciple there whom he loved, he said to his mother, 'Woman, behold, your son.' Then he said to the disciple, 'Behold, your mother.' And from that hour the disciple took her into his home" (John 19:26-27).

The Church has always seen the disciple John as representing us at the foot of the Cross, so when Jesus told him that Mary was to be his mother (bear in mind that John's mother, Salome, was also there at the Cross), He was making clear that Mary was to be the mother of us all. In his encyclical *Mother of the Redeemer*, Pope John Paul II explained it this way:

> "The words uttered by Jesus from the Cross signify that the motherhood of her who bore Christ finds a 'new' continuation in the Church and through the Church, symbolized and represented by John. In this way, she who as the one 'full of grace' was brought into the mystery of Christ in order to be his mother and thus the Holy Mother of God, through the Church remains in that mystery as 'the woman' spoken of by the Book of Genesis (3:15) at the beginning and by the Apocalypse (12:1) at the end of the history of salvation.
>
> "In accordance with the eternal plan of Providence, Mary's divine motherhood is to be poured out upon the Church, as indicated by statements of Tradition, according

to which Mary's 'motherhood' of the Church is the reflection and extension of her motherhood of the Son of God" (n. 24).

Q. Can you respond to those who say that Jesus "rebuked" His Mother three times in the Gospels?

A. First of all, there is no way that Jesus would rebuke or dishonor His mother in violation of the Fourth Commandment. But, second, if we look at each instance, we will see that Jesus was not rebuking His mother, but was actually holding her up for praise. For example, in Matthew 12:46-50, Jesus told a person who said that His mother and brothers were outside, "Who is my mother? Who are my brothers?" Christ then pointed to His disciples and said, "Here are my mother and my brothers. For whoever does the will of my heavenly Father is my brother, and sister, and mother."

Who was Jesus' first and greatest disciple? His mother. Who was the first person to hear the word of God and to do the will of His heavenly Father? His mother. While some of Jesus' kin abandoned Him, His mother remained faithful all the way to the Cross. Jesus was presenting Mary as a model for imitation, not as an object of rebuke.

The same is true in Luke 11:27-28, when a woman in the crowd said to Jesus, "Blessed is the womb that carried you and the breasts at which you nursed." Our Lord replied, "Rather, blessed are those who hear the word of God and observe it." By the way, the Greek word for "rather" is *menoun*, which really means "yes, but in addition" or "further." Thus, Christ was saying that His mother was blessed in a unique way in that she carried the Savior, but further blessed are those who hear the word of God and keep it.

The third occasion was at the wedding feast in Cana, when Mary told Jesus that the wine had run out and He said, "Woman, how does your concern affect me?" (John 2:4).

Mary did not take this as a rebuke, but rather as an invitation to go to the chief steward and tell him to do whatever her Son asked. If Jesus were rebuking His mother, would He have honored her request by performing the miracle of changing water into wine? He was showing us that we also can seek Mary's intercession with Him.

Q. What do we mean by the Assumption of the Blessed Virgin Mary?

A. The Assumption of Mary, which means that she was taken directly to Heaven, body and soul, at the end of her life, is the corollary to her Immaculate Conception. The reasoning behind this dogma is that, since Mary was free from Original Sin, and the corruption of the body in the grave is a consequence of that sin, she did not suffer the decay of the grave. It is not unreasonable to say that Jesus would want His mother to share in His bodily glorification since it was her body that sheltered Him for nine months.

Publicly stated belief in this doctrine can be traced back at least to the sixth century, when St. Gregory of Tours wrote that the Lord Jesus came to earth at the end of Mary's life and commanded that her holy body "be taken in a cloud into Paradise, where now, rejoined to the soul, it rejoices with the Lord's chosen ones, and is in the enjoyment of the good of an eternity that will never end."

St. Robert Bellarmine (1542-1621) also explained the rationale for the Assumption of Mary in these words:

> "And who, I ask, could believe that the ark of holiness, the dwelling place of the Word of God, the temple of the Holy Spirit, could be reduced to ruin? My soul is filled with horror at the thought that the virginal flesh which had begotten God, had brought Him into the world, had nourished and carried Him, could have been turned into ashes or given over to be food for worms."

There is also a negative proof for her Assumption in that neither her tomb nor her remains were ever found. It was commonplace in the early Church to venerate the bones and resting places of the saints, but there is no historical record of such veneration of the Virgin Mary. That is because there were no bodily remains to venerate, and the faithful knew that from the earliest days of the Church.

But it wasn't until 1950, however, that Pope Pius XII, after consulting with bishops all over the world, infallibly proclaimed as a divinely revealed dogma, "that the Immaculate Mother of God, the ever-Virgin Mary, having completed the course of her earthly life, was assumed body and soul into heavenly glory."

Q. Has the Church ever said whether the Virgin Mary died before she was assumed into Heaven?

A. The Church has never formally declared that the Blessed Mother died before she was assumed, body and soul, into Heaven, but saints, holy writers, and Popes have said that she underwent death but not the decay of the grave. For example, St. John Damascene (675-749) referred to an "ancient and most truthful tradition" that Mary did die and was placed in a coffin in the Garden of Gethsemane. After three days of singing and chanting by angels, the coffin was opened, but the Apostles "were unable anywhere to find her most lauded body."

And Pope Pius XII, in his proclamation of the Assumption, said that the Fathers and Doctors of the Church, in their explanations of the meaning of the Assumption, brought "into sharper light the fact that this feast shows, not only that the dead body of the Blessed Virgin Mary remained incorrupt, but that she gained a triumph out of death, her heavenly glorification after the example of her only begotten Son, Jesus Christ" (*Munificentissimus Deus*, n. 20).

In a homily for the Assumption that appeared in the July 2007 *Homiletic & Pastoral Review*, Fr. William Martin offered these eloquent thoughts on the end of our Lady's life:

> "The death which was long desired came at length to her who was the mother of the living. But death came not as a punishment of sin, but almost as a privilege, so that she could be united to her Son in all things in the redemption of the world. Mary died not of sickness, nor was her death a tragic one. Our Blessed Mother died of love. Her burning love of God actually consumed her natural strength. Her death was a holocaust of love, a love so great that the earth could not contain it, a love so ardent that it broke loose from its bodily chains and flew to its God. And all Heaven rejoiced at the reunion of Mother and Son. God decreed from all eternity that the body which was once the home for God on earth would return at death to the home of God in Heaven, where she with Christ could continue her office as mediatrix."

Q. On what basis does the Church call Mary Queen of Heaven and Earth, as in the fifth Glorious Mystery?

A. While the fifth Glorious Mystery – the Crowning of Mary as Queen of Heaven and Earth – is not specifically mentioned in the Bible, Mary's Queenship in Heaven makes sense if we look at the role of the queen-mother in the Old Testament. Virtually every time a new king is introduced in First and Second Kings, his mother is mentioned (e.g., 1 Kings 14:21, 15:2, 22:42). Many kings had multiple wives, making it difficult to choose one to be queen, so the king's mother was given the title and role.

Consider, for example, the role of Bathsheba, the wife of David and the mother of Solomon. When David was king and Bathsheba entered his presence, she bowed to the floor in homage to him and said, "May my lord, King David, live forever!" (1 Kings 1:31). But after David died and Solomon became king, Bathsheba went directly to him to ask a favor, and when she entered the room, Solomon "stood up to meet her and paid her homage. Then he sat down upon his throne, and a throne was provided for the king's mother, who sat at his right" (1 Kings 2:19).

Bathsheba no longer pays homage to the king; he pays homage to her, and he seats her on his right, the position of authority. When she told Solomon that she had a small favor to ask of him, the king said, "Ask it, my mother ... for I will not refuse you" (1 Kings 2:20).

Jesus did not use these same words when His mother told Him at Cana that the wine had run out, but He deferred to her wishes and performed a miracle at her request, even though His hour had not yet come. He continues to defer to the wishes of His mother and queen in Heaven. Thus, the *Catechism* says (n. 966) that when Mary's earthly life was finished, she was " 'taken up body and soul into heavenly glory, and exalted by the Lord as Queen over all things, so that she might be the more fully conformed to her Son, the Lord of lords and conqueror of sin and death' " [*LG* 59; cf. Pius XII, *Munificentissimus Deus* (1950): DS 3903; cf. Rev 19:16].

Summarizing Catholic belief, Dr. Ludwig Ott said in his book *Fundamentals of Catholic Dogma* that "Mary's right to reign as Queen of Heaven is a consequence of her Divine Motherhood. Since Christ, because of the hypostatic union, is as man the Lord and King above all creation (cf. Lk. 1:32f.; Apc. 19:16), so Mary as 'the Mother of the Lord' (Lk. 1:43) shares in the royal dignity of her Son, even if only in an analogical way.

"Furthermore, Mary's royal merit is based on her intrinsic connection with Christ in His work of Redemption. Just as Christ is also our Lord and King because He has redeemed us with His precious Blood (1 Cor. 6:20; 1 Pet. 1:18f.), so, in an analogical way, Mary is our Lady and Queen because she, the new Eve, has shared intimately in the redemptive work of Christ, the new Adam, by suffering with Him and offering Him up to the Eternal Father. Mary's sublime dignity as the Queen of Heaven and Earth makes her supremely powerful in her maternal intercession for her children on earth" (p. 211).

Q. Is it proper to recite the rosary with the intention of "making reparation" to the Blessed Mother for the offenses committed against her Immaculate Heart? Isn't God the only one entitled to reparation?

A. Actually, if you stop to think about it, human beings are entitled to reparation, too, in certain circumstances. We are called to make reparation to others for personal sins against justice (by restoring stolen goods or their value) and truth (by correcting the harm done to a person's good name). This kind of reparation is called restitution.

When we make reparation for sins against God, it is called satisfaction. Thus, the penance given by the priest in Confession is called satisfaction since it is an attempt to make amends for our sins. It is a participation in the ultimate act of satisfaction, the death of Christ on the cross. So if we can make reparation for sins against God and against persons in our own lives, why can't we make reparation to the Immaculate Heart of Our Lady, as she requested at Fatima when she spelled out the conditions for fulfilling the First Saturday devotion?

The Rosary of Our Lady

Chapter 3

Marian Devotions

Q. Why do Catholics pray to the Virgin Mary? Shouldn't they pray directly to Jesus?

A. Catholics, of course, do pray directly to Jesus, and to the Father, and to the Holy Spirit, and they certainly regard Jesus as the one, unique mediator between God and us. They would never place Mary on the same level of mediation as Christ, but there is no reason why Mary, who is united in Heaven with Christ, cannot cooperate with Him in bringing people to God.

After noting that the Church's teaching on Mary and her intercessory role can be found in paragraphs 52-69 of Vatican II's *Lumen Gentium*, Pope John Paul II's encyclical *Mother of the Redeemer*, and paragraphs 963-975 of the *Catechism*, we need to acknowledge Mary's unique place in our salvation. She said yes to becoming the Mother of God, gave us at Cana the important admonition, "Do whatever he tells you" (John 2:5), accepted at the foot of the Cross the role of spiritual mother to all of us, and devoted herself in prayer with the leaders of the early Church.

As one who willingly cooperated with her Son's mission of salvation on earth, Mary did not abandon this saving role when she was taken up to Heaven. She is still the Mother of Christ, who showed such a willingness on earth to grant her every request. How better can we ask a favor of Jesus than by presenting it through Mary's hands? In the words of *Lumen Gentium:*

> "By her maternal charity, Mary cares for the brethren of her Son who still journey on earth surrounded by dangers and difficulties, until they are led to their happy fatherland" (n. 62).

The Fathers of Vatican II urged the faithful to "pour forth persevering prayer to the Mother of God and Mother of men. Let them implore that she who aided the beginnings of the Church by her prayers may now, exalted as she is in Heaven above all the saints and angels, intercede with her Son in the fellowship of all the saints" (*Lumen Gentium*, n. 69).

Q. Can you explain further how Mary acts as a go-between in bringing our petitions to God?

A. We once read a homily on this subject by an Army Chaplain named Fr. Edward Hartmann. Here is what he said:

> "Once there was a kingdom whose king was beloved by all. Now there was a farmer in the kingdom who had an apple orchard. Because of his great love for the king, every year the farmer picked the best, the reddest, and the biggest apples and presented them as a gift to the king. The king always praised the farmer for his beautiful apples and for his generosity.
>
> "It came to pass that one year was especially hot and dry and pests infested the farmer's orchard. Even the best apples were small and wrinkled and cracked. The farmer could not find one apple that did not have a worm, and he was very anxious because he did not want to give the king such poor apples.
>
> "The farmer took his gift of apples to the queen and explained his problem. The queen accepted the apples and carefully cut out every blemish from them. She then cut the apples into beautiful thin wedges, just the way the king liked them for dessert.
>
> "When the time was right, the queen presented the apples to the king on behalf of the farmer. When the king ate one of the wedges, he said, 'By far, these apples are the finest gift this farmer has ever given. May he be greatly blessed!'

"In the same way," [said Fr. Hartmann], "Mary takes our imperfect and stained human intentions and presents them to the Father, not as we presented them to her, but cleaned and perfected."

Q. But don't prayers to Mary diminish prayers to God?

A. Not at all. St. Paul asked that "supplications, prayers, petitions, and thanksgivings be offered for everyone" and said that "this is good and pleasing to God our savior" (1 Timothy 2:1,3). If we follow Paul's advice and ask Christians here on earth to pray for us, which we do all the time, why can't we ask Mary and the other Christians in Heaven to pray for us as well?

St. James tells us that "the fervent prayer of a righteous person is very powerful" (James 5:16), and who is more righteous than Mary and the saints in Heaven, those whom the Letter to the Hebrews describes as "the spirits of the just made perfect" (Hebrews 12:23)? Who is closer to God than the Blessed Virgin Mary, whose intercessory prayer to her Son resulted in the miracle at Cana, and the saints, who place "the prayers of the holy ones" before the throne of God (cf. Revelation 5:8)? Why would God not listen to prayers from these holy ones whose saintly lives on earth must have pleased Him greatly?

Q. But how can people who are dead hear our prayers?

A. But those in Heaven aren't dead; in fact, they are more alive now than when they lived on earth. Remember the words of Jesus to the Sadducees:

> "Have you not read in the Book of Moses, in the passage about the bush, how God told him, 'I am the God of Abraham, [the] God of Isaac, and [the] God of Jacob'? He is not God of the dead but of the living. You are greatly misled" (Mark 12:26-27).

Or recall the time that Jesus appeared on the Mount of Transfiguration with Moses and Elijah (cf. Luke 9:28-36). Were these two great saints of the Old Testament dead, or were they very much alive as they conversed with Christ about His coming death in Jerusalem?

In summary, let us note that, in his book *Catholicism and Fundamentalism* (cf. p. 265), Karl Keating included the following comments on prayers to those in Heaven from a book by Orestes Brownson, an American Catholic intellectual who wrote in the mid-nineteenth century:

> "But still it is asked what need to pray to the saints at all, and why not pray directly to God himself, since He is infinitely nearer to us, and more ready and able to help us than any saint is or can be? In reply, I answer that Catholics do pray directly to God, and perhaps even more than they do who reject prayers to the saints, and I might ask, in our turn, why pray even directly to God, since He knows all our wants better than we ourselves know them, knows what we are going to pray for before the prayer is formed in our own heart, and is infinitely more willing to help us than we are to ask his help? The same principle that justifies prayer to God justifies prayers to the saints to intercede for us."

And the same thing can be said about prayers to the Blessed Virgin Mary.

Q. How can Mary really be aware of and respond to all the prayers directed to her?

A. Without denying the importance of direct prayer to God, one can make a strong case for this because she is part of the Communion of Saints, that community of believers made up of the Triumphant Church in Heaven, the Suffering Church in Purgatory, and the Pilgrim Church on earth. We are all part of this spiritual community, and we try to help each other with our prayers. Just because someone is in Heaven does not mean that he or she is beyond our reach. Those in Heaven are alive (cf. 1 Corinthians 15:22) and are just as interested in our well-being as when they were on earth.

Again we turn to Orestes Brownson, this time to answer the statement that Mary and the saints cannot hear our prayers (cf. his book *Saint Worship*, pp. 51-54):

> "But wherefore can they not hear us? Are they not living men and women – even more living than when they tabernacled with us?... There can be no communion where there is no medium of communication. We who live have a medium of communication with those who have gone to their reward and therefore form one communion with them. This medium is Christ Himself, who is the head of every man, and whose life is the life of all who have been begotten anew by the Holy Ghost....
>
> "There being a medium of communication between us and the saints, and they and we forming only one communion, one Body of our Lord, being members of Him and members of one another, nothing can be more reasonable, more natural even, than that we should invoke their prayers, and that they should intercede for us."

Q. Didn't the Second Vatican Council discourage devotion to the Virgin Mary?

A. No, Vatican II continued the ancient Church practice of encouraging devotion to the Blessed Virgin. For example, the Council specifically directed that "practices and exercises of devotion to her be treasured as recommended by the teaching authority of the Church in the course of centuries, and that those decrees issued in earlier times regarding the veneration of images of Christ, the Blessed Virgin, and the saints be religiously observed" (*Lumen Gentium*, n. 67).

Two years later, Pope Paul VI declared in his letter *Christi Matri Rosarii* that this passage from Vatican II "clearly referred to the rosary," the greatest of all devotions to Mary. And he urged "devout recitation of the rosary" as a practice "well-suited to God's people, acceptable to the Mother of God, and powerful in obtaining gifts from Heaven."

Q. Can you summarize the history and origins of the rosary and the mysteries? What role did St. Dominic play?

A. Not all sources agree on the origin of the rosary and the mysteries. Writing in the 1907 edition of the *Catholic Encyclopedia,* Herbert Thurston, S.J., said that "we have positive evidence that both the invention of the beads as a counting apparatus and also the practice of repeating a hundred and fifty *Aves* cannot be due to St. Dominic because they are both notably older than his time. Further, we are assured that the meditating upon the mysteries was not introduced until two hundred years after his death [in 1221]."

On the other hand, St. Louis Mary de Montfort (1673-1716) said that the Blessed Virgin gave the rosary in its present form to St. Dominic in 1214 "as a powerful means of converting the Albigensians and other sinners." In his book *The Secret of the Rosary*, which Pope John Paul II called "an excellent work on the rosary" (cf. his 2002 apostolic letter *The Rosary of the Virgin Mary*, n. 8), de Montfort said that the Blessed Mother appeared to Dominic in a forest near Toulouse in France where he was praying fervently and doing penances for the conversion of the Albigensians, who denied the Sacraments and the hierarchy of the Church.

"Dear Dominic," our Lady said, "do you know which weapon the Blessed Trinity wants to use to reform the world?"

"Oh, my Lady," answered Dominic, "you know far better than I do because next to your Son Jesus Christ you have always been the chief instrument of our salvation."

Mary replied: "I want you to know that, in this kind of

warfare, the battering ram has always been the Angelic Psalter which is the foundation of the New Testament. Therefore, if you want to reach these hardened souls and win them over to God, preach my psalter." (The rosary was called the Angelic Psalter because the 150 recitations of the Angel Gabriel's greeting to Mary ("Hail, full of grace") equaled the number of Psalms in the Old Testament.)

De Montfort got his information from a Dominican named Alan de la Roche (or Alan de Rupe), who wrote late in the 15th century and helped to found the first rosary confraternities. Alan claimed that the rosary predated St. Dominic, but that the saint was responsible for reviving the devotion after his vision of Mary. Alan also said that the Blessed Mother told him in a vision that "it is a very beautiful, profitable prayer ... to recite the Angelic Salutation 150 times. But more pleasing to me, and much more profitable, is the Angelic Salutation when it is combined with meditation on the life, passion, and glory of Jesus Christ, for meditation is the soul of this prayer."

Whatever the facts about whether the rosary originated with St. Dominic, and this view has been endorsed in many official papal statements, it is not implausible to suggest that he was responsible for the basic idea of uniting the saying of Hail Marys with meditation on the mysteries of our Redemption. In the words of one author:

> "The saint's celebrated sermons on the chief mysteries of our salvation, sermons not abstract but concrete in character, were for his hearers so many meditations on those mysteries, before and in between which he was wont, it is surmised, to invite the congregation to recite Hail Marys in order to obtain the divine blessing. If so, was not the most fundamental aspect of the future rosary already at hand, and should not St. Dominic be credited with authorship of the substance of our devotion?" (Msgr. George W. Shea, "The Dominican Rosary," an essay in the anthology entitled *Mariology*, p. 116).

Q. Aren't there some historical examples of the power of the rosary in the history of the Church?

A. Yes, there are the overthrow of the Albigensian heresy mentioned above in the 13th century and the stunning defeat of the Muslim Turks at Lepanto on October 7, 1571, which saved Europe from being overrun by Muslim armies.

The Muslim Turks had for decades been waging a war of conquest on Christendom in the Mediterranean region and had launched a campaign against the port city of Venice. The leaders of the city formed an alliance with Pope St. Pius V and King Philip II of Spain to defend themselves, and the Pope pleaded with Catholics to pray the rosary and to ask the Blessed Mother to beg her Son to bring about victory over the Muslims.

Under the leadership of Philip's half-brother, 24-year-old Don Juan of Austria, who had given every man in his fleet a rosary, the outnumbered allies killed over 30,000 Turks, captured or sank nearly all of the 300 Turkish ships, and freed more than 10,000 Christian galley slaves. At the height of the five-hour battle, Pius V stood up at a meeting in Rome, went and looked out the window in the direction of the battle many miles away, and was given a vision of the victory by the Blessed Mother. He turned to those at the meeting and said, "Let us no longer occupy ourselves with business, but let us go to thank the Lord. The Christian fleet has obtained victory."

Two years later, Pope Gregory XIII instituted a special feast of Our Lady of the Rosary to mark the victory, and that feast has been celebrated ever since on October 7th.

Q. What can we tell someone who scoffs at the rosary as a devotion only for old people or for the illiterate?

A. You can tell them the story of the university student who found himself sharing a train compartment in France with an old man whose shabby clothes and unkempt appearance gave him the look of a French peasant. When the youth noticed the rosary beads in the old man's hands, he remarked contemptuously, "I see you still believe in that medieval fetish, the rosary beads, and I guess you still hold to the Virgin Mary and all the superstitious nonsense that priests tell you."

"Yes, my boy," the man said with a pained expression, "I do believe it all. Don't you?" The student laughed, "Are you serious, old man? Me believe in prayer and such religious hogwash? I should say not. I learned different at college ... and if you're smart you'll throw those silly beads away and learn something about the new thought."

"The new thought?" the old man said with tears in his eyes. "I'm afraid I don't understand. Perhaps you could help me."

The young man softened a bit and seemed to take pity on his traveling companion. "Well, if you can read," he said, "I'd be glad to send you some of my literature. You do read?"

The old man nodded, "I read a little when I am not too busy."

"Splendid!" the college student exclaimed. "To what address shall I send it?"

Reaching into his pocket, the man who looked like a peasant drew out a card and handed it to the youth. The name printed on the card was that of Louis Pasteur, the famous French chemist who developed vaccines against hydrophobia and anthrax and discovered a way to sterilize milk.

Q. But aren't the repetitive prayers of the rosary the kind of repetition that was forbidden by Jesus in Matthew 6:7?

A. In the Scripture passage mentioned, Jesus told His listeners that when praying, "do not babble like the pagans, who think that they will be heard because of their many words" (the King James Bible uses the expression "vain repetitions").

But Jesus was not talking about prayers like the rosary, but rather was criticizing "the hypocrites, who love to stand and pray in the synagogues and on street corners so that others may see them" (Matthew 6:5). Those people just rattled off words with no thought to what they were saying. Reciting the prayers of the rosary, on the other hand, involves meditating on the Joyful, Luminous, Sorrowful, and Glorious events in the life of our Lord and His Mother.

Furthermore, repetitious prayer is not wrong or vain if it is sincere. Jesus Himself repeated the same prayer over and over during His Agony in the Garden of Gethsemane, when He three times asked His Father to "let this cup pass from me" (Matthew 26:39, 42, 44). And Christ told us that the humble tax collector, who kept repeating, "O God, be merciful to me a sinner," went home from the Temple "justified," while the self-righteous and long-winded Pharisee did not (cf. Luke 18:9-14).

The same is true of the many repetitious phrases in Psalm 150, for example, which Jesus must have prayed many times in the synagogues of Nazareth and elsewhere.

Q. How do we answer those who say that reciting the rosary shows that Catholics favor Mary over God since prayers to her outnumber prayers to God by a margin of ten to one?

A. You could point out that at the heart of each Hail Mary is Jesus; that each decade of the rosary concludes with a prayer of praise to the Father, Son, and Holy Spirit and the Fatima prayer ("O my Jesus, forgive us our sins..."); and that all of the twenty mysteries upon which one is supposed to meditate while saying the Hail Marys involve Jesus either explicitly or implicitly.

Even though He is not mentioned in the Descent of the Holy Spirit on the Apostles, it was Jesus who told the Apostles to wait in Jerusalem for the coming of the Holy Spirit (cf. Acts 1:4-5). Nor is He mentioned in the fourth and fifth Glorious Mysteries, but who else would be taking His mother to Heaven at the end of her earthly life or crowning her as Queen of Heaven and Earth?

And can God really be unhappy when Catholics pray the Hail Mary, since He is the author of the prayer that came from the lips of His messenger, the Angel Gabriel, and from the lips of Elizabeth, who was inspired by the Holy Spirit to say what she did?

But the accusation is also groundless since Catholics recognize that Mary always points us to Jesus, as when she said at the wedding feast in Cana: "Do whatever he tells you" (John 2:5).

Q. Has the Fatima ejaculation ("O my Jesus, forgive us our sins …") been officially approved by the Vatican?

A. This prayer was given by our Blessed Lady to the three children in Fatima after they were shown a vision of Hell on July 13, 1917. "You have seen Hell where the souls of poor sinners go," our Lady told the children. "In order to save them, God wishes to establish in the world devotion to my Immaculate Heart." She also said that "when you pray the rosary, say after each mystery: 'O my Jesus, forgive us our sins; save us from the fire of Hell. Lead all souls to Heaven, especially those in most need of your mercy.' "

This prayer was authorized by the Vatican's Sacred Apostolic Penitentiary on February 4, 1956.

Curiously, though, Pope John Paul II made no mention of the Fatima prayer in his apostolic letter *The Rosary of the Virgin Mary*. He suggested following the announcement of each mystery "with the proclamation of a related biblical passage, long or short, depending on the circumstances" (n. 30); highlighting the name of Jesus in each Hail Mary "by the addition of a clause referring to the mystery being contemplated" (n. 33); and following the Gloria at the end of each decade "by a brief concluding prayer, which varies according to local custom" (n. 35).

The Holy Father said that "the contemplation of the mysteries could better express their full spiritual fruitfulness if an effort were made to conclude each mystery with a prayer for the fruits specific to that particular mystery .... One fine liturgical prayer suggests as much, inviting us to pray that, by meditating on the mysteries of the rosary, we may come to 'imitate what they contain and obtain what they promise.' Such a final prayer could take on a legitimate variety of forms, as indeed it already does. In this way the rosary can be better adapted to different spiritual traditions and different Christian communities" (n. 35).

It is not unreasonable to include among the "legitimate variety" of prayers mentioned by the Holy Father the prayer requested by Our Lady of Fatima on July 13, 1917.

Q. Do you know why Pope John Paul II added the Luminous Mysteries to the rosary?

A. In a 2002 Apostolic Letter (*Rosarium Virginis Mariae*) proclaiming a Year of the Rosary, Pope John Paul II recalled that shortly after his elevation to the Chair of Peter in October 1978, "I frankly admitted: 'The rosary is my favorite prayer.'" He said that he had "set the first year of my pontificate within the daily rhythm of the rosary. Today, as I begin the 25th year of my service as the Successor of Peter, I wish to do the same. How many graces have I received in these years from the Blessed Virgin through the rosary: *Magnificat anima mea Dominum!* I wish to lift up my thanks to the Lord in the words of His Most Holy Mother, under whose protection I have placed my Petrine ministry: *Totus Tuus!* (n. 2)."

Later in the letter, the Holy Father expressed his belief that the "Christological depth of the rosary" could be brought out more fully by adding "the mysteries of Christ's public ministry between His Baptism and His Passion," and he proposed five "Mysteries of Light": The Baptism of Jesus in the Jordan, His Self-Manifestation at the Wedding in Cana, His Proclamation of the Kingdom of God, His Transfiguration on the Mountain, and His Institution of the Holy Eucharist at the Last Supper (cf. n. 21).

John Paul said that recitation of the Luminous Mysteries was being "left to the freedom of individuals and communities" and suggested when they might be prayed:

> "If we consider that the 'Glorious Mysteries' are said on both Saturday and Sunday, and that Saturday has always had a special Marian flavor, the second weekly meditation on the 'Joyful Mysteries,' mysteries in which Mary's presence is especially pronounced, could be moved to Saturday. Thursday would then be free for meditating on the 'Mysteries of Light' " (n. 38).

The Luminous Mysteries are wonderful for meditation and prayer because they can inspire us to bring the light of Christ into a world darkened by sin and because they can point us to the necessity of leading a good sacramental life. These mysteries provide an opportunity for meditation and catechesis on Baptism and its necessity for salvation; on Matrimony, the sacrament that signifies the love of God for His Church; on Penance and Reconciliation if we are to be faithful members of the Kingdom; on Anointing of the Sick to prepare us for eternal life; and on the Holy Eucharist, the "Bread from Heaven" that gives us the spiritual nourishment to strengthen us along the journey.

Consider the following opportunities for meditation that are provided by the Luminous Mysteries:

The Baptism of Jesus in the Jordan allows us to meditate on the character and courage of John the Baptist, the identification of Jesus as the "Lamb of God," the first manifestation of the Blessed Trinity, and the sinless Jesus allowing John to baptize Him so as to identify Himself with sinful humanity and to start His journey toward the Cross in

Jerusalem, just as our Baptism started our journey toward the heavenly Jerusalem.

The Wedding Feast at Cana enables us to think about the role of the Blessed Mother in salvation history and how she always points us to Jesus with her famous last words, "Do whatever he tells you"; her identification with the "woman" of Genesis 3:15, the "woman" at the foot of the Cross, and the "woman" of Revelation 12:1; her ability to persuade her Son to perform a miracle even though His "hour" had not yet come; the divine institution of marriage as the union of one man and one woman; and the willingness of Jesus to help married couples when the wine of love has run out of their marriages.

The Proclamation of the Kingdom permits us to focus on the many parables of Jesus about the coming of His Kingdom (cf. chapter 13 of Matthew), as well as to refute the false "Rapture" theory about a secret or invisible Second Coming of Christ and to debunk predictions of the future attributed to Nostradamus, but in fact conjured up long after his death, such as those which try to link his sayings with the events of September 11, 2001.

The Transfiguration on the Mountain brings us back to the experience of Moses in the glorious presence of God (cf. Exodus 34:29-35) and then forward to his and Elijah's conversation with a glorified Jesus in front of Peter, James, and John, thus indicating to the Apostles that the horrors of Good Friday would be followed by the glories of Easter Sunday. It also gives us a foretaste of how our bodies will be transfigured in Heaven at the end of the world.

The Institution of the Holy Eucharist also points us back to the Old Testament feeding of the Israelites in the desert with bread from Heaven (cf. Exodus 16:4-15), then forward to Jesus' feeding of more than 5,000 with five loaves of bread, and forward again to the Last Supper when Jesus promised to give us the true Bread from Heaven that comes to us every time a priest says, "This is my body." This allows us to reflect on the recent example of Iraqi Catholics in the town of Mosul, who continued to attend Mass in the face of deadly terrorist bombings because, in their words, "Without the Eucharist, we cannot live." This should also lead us to pray for the many Catholics known to all of us who seem quite content to live without the Eucharist.

Q. Is it still proper to recite the rosary at the wake or viewing of a dead person?

A. Older Catholics can remember when the rosary was always recited at wakes, but in recent times the vigil rite for the deceased has been changed to a Scripture service. This is the Church's official prayer for the deceased, and the priest is obligated to celebrate it, either in the form of the Liturgy of the Word or the appropriate Office of the Dead.

Since this service takes a while, adding a rosary would extend the period of prayer and perhaps cause congestion at a crowded wake, so the rosary is not being said as the principal prayer at the funeral home.

However, this should not be seen as a downgrading of the rosary, which remains an honored non-liturgical prayer. What is being done today is to have a family member of the deceased lead the rosary just before visiting hours begin.

Q. What is the Little Office of the Blessed Virgin?

A. According to Fr. Jovian Lang's *Dictionary of the Liturgy,* the Little Office of the Blessed Virgin developed as a private devotion in the 11th century, was later adopted by several congregations of religious women in place of the Divine Office after the Council of Trent in the 16th century, is considered part of the public prayer of the Church by decision of the Second Vatican Council, and was revised in English as recently as 1988.

Patterned after the Liturgy of the Hours, the Little Office is comprised of seven hours and features biblical texts referring directly or indirectly to Mary, as well as variable Psalms with proper antiphons, responsories, intercessions, and prayers – all in a Marian vein.

"Its originality," says the *Dictionary of the Liturgy,* "lies precisely in this emphasis given to the person of Mary, who nonetheless never appears in isolated fashion. She is always portrayed as part of the history of salvation, as the admirable fruit of the Divine Power, as the Mother of the Lord, or as the image of the Church. Hence, the Little Office is a way of living – in praise and reflection – the principal moments of each day with Mary, who spent her life alongside her Son in ardent love, in joyous praise, and in deep faith" (p. 329).

Q. What is the history of the Legion of Mary?

A. The Legion of Mary is an association of clergy and laity that was founded by Frank Duff in Ireland in 1921. According to its handbook, the object of the Legion "is the glory of God through the sanctification of its members by prayer and active cooperation, under ecclesiastical guidance, in Mary's and the Church's work of crushing the head of the serpent and advancing the reign of Christ."

The spirit of the Legion, the handbook says, "is that of Mary herself ... her profound humility, her perfect obedience, her angelical sweetness, her continual prayer, her universal mortification, her altogether spotless purity, her heroic patience, her heavenly wisdom, her self-sacrificing courageous love of God, and, above all, her faith – that virtue which has in her alone been found in its utmost extent and never equaled" (p. 4).

The Legion of Mary was established in the United States in 1931, and thousands of local units (known as praesidiums) currently carry on their devotional and apostolic work here and throughout the world. They foster the spiritual growth of their members and also send them out to visit fallen-away Catholics and non-Catholics.

Q. Do you know the meaning of the phrase "terrible as an army set in battle array" that appears in the prayer *Catena Legionis* of the Legion of Mary?

A. The phrase refers to the Blessed Virgin and is part of an antiphon recited by those who belong to the Legion before and after recitation of the Magnificat. The reason for the metaphor can be found in their official handbook:

> "The Legion of Mary is an association of Catholics who, with the sanction of the Church and under the powerful leadership of Mary Immaculate, Mediatrix of All Graces (who is fair as the moon, bright as the sun and – to Satan and his legionaries – terrible as an army set in battle array), have formed themselves into a legion for service in the warfare which is perpetually waged by the Church against the world and its evil powers" (p. 1).

The Legion takes its name from the Roman Legion and seeks to inspire in its members the same spirit of "submission to authority, an unflagging sense of duty, perseverance in the face of obstacles, endurance in hardship, and loyalty to the cause in the tiniest details of duty" – only "supernaturalized and tempered and sweetened by contact with her [Mary] who can best teach the secret of loving, gracious service" (p. 269).

Q. What can you tell us about the scapulars that are worn by many Catholics?

A. In the beginning, scapulars were part of the habit of religious orders. Resembling an apron, they were originally shoulder-wide strips of cloth worn over the tunic and reaching almost to the feet in front and behind. They came to symbolize the cross and yoke of Christ and now consist of two small squares of cloth joined by strings and worn about the neck as a sign of a person's association with a religious order and for devotional purposes.

The Church has approved the scapular as a sacramental, i.e., a holy object that can bring spiritual benefits to its user. Unlike the Sacraments, which produce grace by virtue of the rite itself, the efficacy of sacramentals depends on the devotion, faith, and love of those who use them.

During an appearance in 1251 to St. Simon Stock, the Prior General of the Carmelite Order, the Blessed Virgin Mary promised that all those who wear the brown Carmelite scapular "shall not suffer eternal fire and, if wearing it they die, they shall be saved." This does not mean, of course, that one could deliberately lead a sinful life and expect to benefit from the scapular promise since that would constitute a sin of presumption. Furthermore, if one believed that the cloth itself was a guarantee of Heaven, that would be superstitious, but that is not what Catholics believe.

Just as a person might wear a mother's ring or a father's watch as a reminder of a loved one, so one can wear a scapular or other religious object as a reminder of our eternal destination in Heaven, and our responsibility to live in such a way as to reach that destination.

Seven centuries after the appearance to St. Simon Stock, Pope Pius XI put the promise in perspective when he cautioned the faithful that, "although it is very true that the Blessed Virgin loves all who love her, nevertheless those who wish to have the Blessed Mother as a helper at the hour of death must in life merit such a signal favor by abstaining from sin and laboring in her honor."

The Church recognizes some 20 scapulars for devotional use, with five of the major ones being those of Our Lady of Mount Carmel (brown), the Passion (red), the Seven Dolors (black), the Immaculate Conception (blue), and the Holy Trinity (white). The Church also recognizes the substitution of a scapular medal for the cloth scapular. It may be worn about the neck or made part of a ring.

Q. What does a scapular medal look like and who authorized it?

A. The scapular medal has a representation of the Sacred Heart on one side and of the Blessed Virgin Mary on the other side. It was authorized by Pope St. Pius X in 1910. Here is the text of the decree issued by the Holy Father:

> "For the future, all the faithful already inscribed or who shall be inscribed in one or the other of the real scapulars approved by the Holy See (excepting those which are proper to the Third Orders) by what is known as regular enrollment may, instead of the cloth scapulars, one or several, wear on their persons, either round the neck or otherwise, provided it be in a becoming manner, a single medal of metal, through which, by the observance of laws laid down for each scapular, they shall be enabled to share in and gain all the spiritual favors (not excepting what is known as the Sabbatine Privilege of the Scapular of Our Lady of Mount Carmel), and all the privileges attached to each."

After declaring that the medal must show the images of the Sacred Heart and the Blessed Virgin Mary on opposite sides, St. Pius said that "it must be blessed with a separate blessing for each of the scapulars in which the person has been enrolled and for which the wearer wishes it to suffice. Finally, these separate blessings may be given by a single sign of the cross, whether in the act of enrollment or in what order they may have taken place; the blessing may be given by a priest other than the one who made the enrollment, as long as he possesses the faculty, ordinary or delegated, of blessing the different scapulars – the limitations, clauses, and conditions attached to the faculty he uses still holding their force – all things to the contrary, even those calling for special mention, notwithstanding."

Q. What is the Sabbatine Privilege?

A. This refers to the promise of our Lady that those who wear the brown scapular will benefit after their death from her continual intercession and her special protection, particularly on Saturdays, the day of the week especially dedicated by the Church to honoring the Blessed Mother. Some have cited a statement allegedly made in 1322 by Pope John XXII, that faithful wearers of the scapular would be released from Purgatory on the Saturday after their death. This statement is surely false, and the correct understanding of the promise was stated in 1613 by Pope Paul V:

> "It is permitted to the Carmelite Fathers to preach that the Christian people may believe that the Blessed Virgin will help by her continued assistance and her merits, particularly on Saturdays, the souls of the members of the Scapular Fraternity who have died in the grace of God, if in their life they had worn the scapular, observed chastity according to their state in life, and recited the Office of the Blessed Virgin or observed the fasts of the Church, practicing abstinence [from meat] on Wednesdays and Saturdays."

In other words, the intercession of Mary will occur "particularly on Saturdays," but not on a particular Saturday.

In a recent letter, the Carmelite Provincial Superiors in the United States and Canada warned against spreading the scapular devotion "with extravagant claims that have no historical background and which sometimes are difficult to reconcile with sound Catholic doctrine." They stated that "in our catechesis of the Brown Scapular of Our Lady of Mount Carmel, we Carmelites accept the mandate to clearly teach the doctrine that the Church teaches and our Carmelite Rule affirms so well – that Jesus Christ is the only one who liberates us from our sin."

Q. Is there an enrollment rite associated with wearing the scapular?

A. Yes, there is a Rite for the Blessing and Enrollment in the Scapular of the Blessed Virgin Mary of Mount Carmel that was approved by the Holy See in 1996. Any priest or deacon has the faculties for blessing the scapular and, once given the authority to act in the name of the Carmelite Order, may receive the faithful into the confraternity of the scapular. According to the *Encyclopedia of Catholic Devotions and Practices*, which was compiled by Ann Ball, here is the prayer for the blessing of a scapular:

> "O God, author and perfection of holiness, who will call those who were born of water and the Holy Spirit to the fullness of the Christian life, look with kindness on those who are about to receive devoutly the Scapular of Carmel which they will wear faithfully as the sign of their commitment to the Virgin Mary of Mount Carmel. Grant that in surrendering to the love of the most tender Virgin, they may conform themselves to the image of Jesus Christ, your Son, and having run the course of this life happily, may they enter into the joy of your house. Through Christ Our Lord. Amen" (p. 516).

The minister then places the scapular on the person to be enrolled and says:

> "Receive this scapular. [Through this scapular you become a member of the Confraternity of the Blessed Virgin Mary of Mount Carmel.] Full of faith in the love of such a great Mother, dedicate yourself to imitating her and to a special relationship with her. Wear this sign as a reminder of the presence of Mary in your daily commitment to be clothed in Jesus Christ and to manifest Him in your life for the good of the Church and the whole of humanity, and to the glory of the Most Blessed Trinity. Amen" (p. 517).

Brown Scapular of Our Lady of Mount Carmel

Chapter 4

Marian Apparitions

Q. Do Catholics have to believe in apparitions of the Virgin Mary?

A. Catholics are only obliged to believe in *public* revelation, which ended with the death of the last Apostle, and in what the Church teaches about the revealed truths we find in Sacred Scripture and Sacred Tradition. The apparitions of our Lord and the Blessed Virgin Mary or the saints to certain individuals come under the heading of *private* revelation, and we are not bound to believe in those apparitions since they are not part of the Deposit of Faith.

The *Catechism* tells us that "throughout the ages, there have been so-called 'private' revelations, some of which have been recognized by the authority of the Church. They do not, however, belong to the deposit of faith. It is not their role to improve or complete Christ's definitive Revelation, but to help live more fully by it during a certain period of history." It is up to the magisterium of the Church, the *Catechism* says, to guide the faithful in knowing "how to discern and welcome in these revelations whatever constitutes an authentic call of Christ or his saints to the Church" (n. 67).

The *Catechism* says that the "Christian faith cannot accept 'revelations' that claim to surpass or correct the Revelation of which Christ is the fulfillment, as is the case in certain non-Christian religions and also in recent sects which base themselves on such 'revelations' " (*Ibid.*).

Catholics may, however, believe in those apparitions which are well-authenticated and have been approved by the Church. "Marian shrines and places of pilgrimage are a kind of 'geography' of faith by which we seek to meet the Mother of God in order to find a strengthening of our Christian life," said Pope John Paul during a visit to San Antonio, Texas, in

1987. He said that "popular devotion to the Blessed Virgin Mary is rooted in sound doctrine."

Recall, too, that recent Popes have also indicated their approval of Marian appearances by making highly publicized visits to these shrines. Pope Paul VI visited Fatima in 1967; Pope John Paul II went there in 1982, exactly one year from the day that he was gravely wounded in St. Peter's Square, to thank Mary for saving his life, and again in 2000 to beatify Francisco and Jacinta, two of the children to whom the Blessed Mother appeared in 1917; and Pope Benedict XVI visited Fatima in 2010.

Q. But didn't Pope John Paul warn against getting too caught up in following apparitions before the Church had pronounced them worthy of belief?

A. Yes, because he feared that putting one's personal opinion ahead of the official determination of the Church could be a recipe for spiritual disaster. In a statement that appeared in *L'Osservatore Romano* on September 18, 1996, the Holy Father was quoted as saying:

> "Some members of the People of God are not rooted firmly enough in the faith, so that the sects, with their deceptive proselytism, mislead them to separate themselves from true communion in Christ. Within the Church community, the multiplication of supposed 'apparitions' or 'visions' is sowing confusion and reveals a certain lack of a solid basis to the faith and Christian life among her members."

In his book *A Still, Small Voice*, Fr. Benedict Groeschel also advised Catholics to keep all claims of heavenly revelations in perspective. He said that "private revelations are not the most important things in the world. The consistent and authentic pursuit of a holy life leading to a loving union with God is the essential element of true religion .... It is important to keep clearly in mind that private revelations have no significance apart from the public revelation of Sacred Scripture, interpreted by the traditional teaching of the Church" (p. 24).

Later in the book, Fr. Groeschel said that one general principle to be followed is that "private revelation by definition is personal and therefore must be carefully applied by those for whom it was meant and only within the limits of ordinary human prudence and never in an unreasonable way or against the teaching of the Church. It must never be considered an infallible guide in any situation" (p. 35).

He also expressed concern about "the revelation addicts," those people who "avidly collect all reports of visions and revelations and are generally willing to be guided by the Church in most matters except for the authority of these visions" (pp. 86-87).

Fr. Groeschel said further (pp. 87-88) that "there are groups of good souls who make themselves sitting ducks, as it were, for the possibility of deception by false revelations. They are too curious. They are addicted to possible revelations. Instead of spiritually imbibing the gentle but strong message of Scripture and even of approved revelations, they weekly or monthly find new ones. I suspect that now and then they may come across an authentic private revelation, but they never have the chance to learn anything from it because they just move on, seeking desperately for some other sign to reassure themselves. They must represent in the contemporary world the same group of people whom Our Lord admonished when He spoke of those who said of the Messiah, 'Here he is, there he is .... He is in the desert' (Mt 24:23-26)."

Q. What do you say to people who argue that the authenticity of a reported apparition can be judged by its fruits, that is, by the numbers of those who return to the Faith and receive the Sacraments after a lapse of many years?

A. In his book *A Still, Small Voice*, Fr. Benedict Groeschel said that he has observed such piety and genuine religious experiences at places associated with revelations. He cautioned, however, that "each person's religious experience stands alone. The fact is that we cannot judge the reported revelation by its fruits. You would be required to take Joseph Smith and the Mormon doctrine very seriously if you went simply by the effects of his revelation. It is responsible for several billion dollars in religious donations every year – and yet very serious questions have been raised by Mormon scholars about the moral life of this 'prophet' " (p. 100).

Fr. Groeschel said that reported revelations can be dismissed if one or more of the following factors is present (cf. pp. 102-104):

* The seer is clearly mentally ill.

* The substance of the revelation is clearly contrary to or inconsistent with the teaching of the Church.

* The attitude of the alleged visionary is "defiant, proud, judgmental, or provocative."

* The seer makes erroneous prophecies.

* The visionary is unable to face the possibility that he or she has been deceived.

* There is evidence that the reported revelation or the recipient "is involved in magic, the occult, or the diabolical."

The priest said that "no one should feel guilty about being cautious, even if one is positively disposed to the message or the revelation. Intelligence, judgment, and discernment are all gifts of God and should be used .... If time proves the revelation authentic, false, or ultimately doubtful, the person who has followed a reasonable middle road will have served the Kingdom of God well" (p. 105-106).

Q. Are there any similarities in the various approved apparitions of the Blessed Mother?

A. In a book he edited, entitled *A Woman Clothed With the Sun,* which summarized eight appearances by the Blessed

Mother (Lourdes, La Salette, Guadalupe, Beauraing, Fatima, Paris, Knock, and Banneux), John J. Delaney noted the following similarities surrounding the apparitions:

One, most of them occurred in isolated areas where religion was under attack, even though the countries were predominantly Catholic.

Two, most of those to whom our Lady appeared were children and those who were adults possessed a simple, childlike faith. They were not the smartest people of their time, but they accepted the fact that the Mother of God had appeared to them, and they passed along her message exactly as she had given it to them. No hostile questioning, or even harassment, could get them to change their stories.

Three, our Lady's appearances were often accompanied by a blinding light whose brilliance did not hurt the eyes of those experiencing the vision and often by water, either a spring in the ground or heavy rain. The visionaries had to endure adverse conditions, such as cold and driving rain.

Four, the Blessed Virgin was always young and beautiful and appeared in clothes of dazzling colors, often blue and gold but always predominantly white.

Five, prayer, penance, and reparation for sin were the constant themes running through the messages of our Lady. Her clear and direct message, said John Delaney, "is simply that God is displeased with what has been going on on this earth. His patience is almost exhausted, and unless we listen to Him through His Blessed Mother He will wreak the vengeance which He has unleashed on the earth before" (p. 31). If people turn away from sin and back to God, said Mary, she will intercede with her Son for us.

In short, said Delaney, "what Mary, the Mother of God and our Blessed Mother, is proposing in all these visitations is so stupendous that the human mind reels at the gigantic implications implicit in her promise. As the mother of us all, she is offering to save the human race from its own folly and is pointing out to us the path we must follow to attain the salvation of our individual eternal souls. Small wonder she weeps so often in these appearances" (p. 34).

Author's Note: What follows are reports of appearances of the Blessed Virgin Mary that have been recounted in books, newspapers, magazines, and Church documents. We have grouped them into three categories: (1) Those that have been officially approved by the Church, (2) those that the Church has declared false and not worthy of belief, and (3) those that are still under investigation as this is written.

Approved Apparitions

Q. What are the facts about the appearances of our Lady to a girl in Banneux, Belgium in 1933?

A. In the winter of 1933, the Virgin Mary appeared eight times to a twelve-year-old girl named Mariette Beco in the desperately poor village of Banneux. The beautiful lady was dressed in a dazzlingly white gown with a sky-blue sash, and a rosary hung on her right arm. When Mariette asked Mary who she was, she replied, "I am the Virgin of the Poor." She prayed the rosary with Mariette, blessed her, and asked that a small chapel be built there.

When word of the apparitions got out, Mariette was taunted by her classmates and even beaten up by a group of boys. The parish priest, Abbe Louis Jamin, had confided to a fellow priest that he wished Heaven would give him a sign that the apparitions were authentic, "for example, if Mariette's father were converted." As he was leaving the Beco house that night, Mr. Beco asked to see him the next day to confess his sins and to receive Communion.

Our Lady's final appearance took place on March 2, 1933, and she told Mariette, "I am the Mother of the Savior,

Mother of God. Pray much." She then stretched forth her hands, blessed Mariette, and said, "Adieu – till we meet in God."

Over the next five years, as the cult to the Virgin of the Poor grew steadily, there were twenty cures that met the strict standards for a miracle. Then, on the Feast of the Immaculate Heart of Mary in 1949, Bishop Louis Joseph Kerkhofs of the Diocese of Liege, after years of investigation by a Belgian commission and by the Vatican, proclaimed the visits by the Blessed Virgin Mary to the village of Banneux in 1933 to be worthy of belief.

Q. Has the Church given her approval to our Lady's appearance at Beauraing, and what was her message?

A. Yes, the Church has given its approval to the apparitions at Beauraing, a village in Belgium where the Blessed Mother appeared thirty-three times to five children from November 29, 1932, to January 3, 1933. Ten years after the last appearance, on February 2, 1943, Bishop Andre-Marie Charue authorized public devotion to "Our Lady of Beauraing."

On July 2, 1949, the Bishop sent a letter to all the priests in his diocese in which he said: "We are able in all serenity and prudence to affirm that the Queen of Heaven appeared to the children of Beauraing during the winter of 1932-1933 especially to show us in her maternal heart the anxious appeal for prayer and the promise of her powerful mediation for the conversion of sinners."

Our Lady of Beauraing is known as the "Virgin with the Golden Heart" because she showed the children a heart of gold. Her messages included an admonition that the children "always be good" and that they "pray, pray very much." She also identified herself as "the Immaculate Virgin," "the Mother of God," and "the Queen of Heaven," and she promised that "I will convert sinners."

Q. Has the Church approved the reported appearances of the Blessed Virgin to a woman in Betania, Venezuela, from 1976 to 1990?

A. Yes, the Church has said that Mary did appear thirty-one times to Maria Esperanza (1928-2004) at her farm two hours outside the capital city of Caracas. Among other things, the Blessed Mother was reported to have said that "the great moment of reconciliation has arrived .... I extend my love to all my children, dwellers on earth, and be loyal to Jesus, so you may discover the wonderful secret of unity ... which will help us find the key to God's kingdom."

After interviewing nearly 500 witnesses and compiling a file of almost 400 written statements, Bishop Pio Bello Ricardo, the bishop of the diocese in which Betania is located, issued this statement on November 21, 1987:

> "Having studied the apparitions of the Virgin Mary at Finca Betania and having prayed assiduously to God for spiritual discernment, I declare that in my judgment the aforementioned apparitions are authentic and supernatural in character. I therefore officially approve that the place where they occurred to be considered a sacred place. May it become a place of pilgrimage, a place of prayer, reflection, and cult."

Because Maria Esperanza died in New Jersey, the Bishop of Metuchen, the Most Reverend Paul Bootkoski, opened her cause for beatification and canonization in January of 2010.

Q. What happened at Fatima in 1917?

A. From May to October of 1917, the Blessed Virgin Mary appeared six times to three shepherd children in the Portuguese village of Fatima. She showed them a vision of Hell, predicted World War II and the rise of Communism in Russia, and promised the conversion of Russia, the end of World War I, and peace in the world if people would pray, especially the rosary, do penance, and make reparation for sin.

At her final appearance on October 13, 1917, the Virgin Mary, after saying that "I am the Lady of the Rosary," gave the children her promised miracle in order to convince the tens of thousands of onlookers present that she had indeed been appearing to the little shepherds and that people should heed her message. What happened that day was described in detail by Avelino de Almeida, an atheistic reporter for the Lisbon newspaper *O Seculo*. He had come to Fatima to prove the claims of the children a hoax, but he could not ignore what he witnessed with his own eyes.

On the front page of the October 15th issue of *O Seculo* was a picture of the children and a headline that read: "Bewildering Happenings! How the Sun Danced at Midday at Fatima." According to the story, and the testimony of eyewitnesses, a heavy rain stopped at noon and the sun came out. The people were able to look directly at the sun without hurting their eyes. As they gazed upward, the sun began to spin on its axis, sending out rays of multicolored light like a giant pinwheel.

The sun then seemed to tear itself loose from the sky and began a mad, zigzag plunge toward earth. People cried out in terror, thinking they were about to die, and begged God for mercy and forgiveness. But then the sun halted its descent and returned to its place in the sky, resuming a normal brightness that prevented people from looking directly at it.

This solar phenomenon was witnessed by over 70,000 people standing in the pasture known as the Cova da Iria, and it was reported in the Lisbon-based newspapers *O Seculo* and *O Dia*. For more details, see John J. Delaney's book *A Woman Clothed With the Sun*, Fr. Joseph Pelletier's book *The Sun Danced at Fatima*, and Tarcisio Cardinal Bertone's book *The Last Secret of Fatima*.

On October 13, 1930, the Bishop of Leiria (now Leiria-Fatima) published a pastoral letter in which he said that "we hereby declare on the strength of the arguments set forth here, as well as of others that we omit for the sake of brevity, that the visions seen by the shepherd children between May 13 and October 13, 1917, in the Cova da Iria, located in the parish of Fatima in this diocese, are worthy of faith. We also hereby authorize the official cult of Our Lady of Fatima."

Q. Who were the children and what happened to them?

A. Our Lady appeared to Lucia dos Santos, ten, and her two cousins, Francisco and Jacinta Marto, ages nine and seven, respectively. The Blessed Mother had said on June 13th that she would take Francisco and Jacinta to Heaven soon, but Lucia would "stay longer" because "Jesus wants to use you to make me known and loved. He wants to establish in the world a devotion to my Immaculate Heart."

When Lucia asked, "Shall I stay here alone," Mary replied: "No, daughter, I shall never leave you. My Immaculate Heart will be your refuge and the way that will lead you to God."

Francisco died in 1919 and Jacinta in 1920, victims of a flu epidemic that killed an estimated twenty million people. (Both were beatified by Pope John Paul II in 2000.) Lucia entered a convent of the Dorothean Sisters in Spain in 1925, received while there a number of visions from the Virgin Mary, and subsequently wrote a four-volume account of the Fatima events.

In 1948, she transferred to a Carmelite convent in Coimbra, Portugal, and remained there until her death in 2005 at the age of 97. She made public appearances during visits to Fatima by Pope Paul VI in 1967 and Pope John Paul II in 1982 and 2000.

Our Lady of Fatima

Q. Didn't Jacinta, shortly before her death, reveal some warnings she had received from the Virgin Mary?

A. In January 1920, a month before she died, Jacinta stayed at a convent in Lisbon with a nun named Mother Godinho, who wrote down everything Jacinta said. According to Jacinta, the Blessed Mother made the following comments about sin, war, and priests and religious:

On sin: "The sins which cause most souls to go to Hell are the sins of the flesh. Fashions will much offend our Lord. People who serve God should not follow the fashions."

On war: "Wars are the punishments for sin. If people amend their lives, our Lord will even yet save the world, but if not, punishment will come."

On priests and religious: "You must pray very much for sinners and for priests and religious. Priests must be very, very pure. Disobedience of priests and religious to their superiors displeases our Lord very much."

Q. Did our Lady really show the children a vision of Hell?

A. Yes, she did during her appearance to them on July 13, 1917. In her memoir of August 31, 1941, Sister Lucia said that the ground opened up in front of them and "our Lady showed us a great sea of fire which seemed to be under the earth. Plunged in this fire were demons and souls in human form, like transparent burning embers, all blackened or burnished bronze, floating about in the conflagration, now raised into the air by the flames that issued from within themselves together with great clouds of smoke, now falling back on every side like sparks in a huge fire, without weight or equilibrium, and amid shrieks and groans of pain and despair, which horrified us and made us tremble with fear. The demons could be distinguished by their terrifying and repulsive likeness to frightful and unknown animals, all black and transparent."

Lucia said that "this vision lasted but an instant. How can we ever be grateful enough to our kind heavenly Mother, who had already prepared us by promising, in the first apparition [in May], to take us to Heaven. Otherwise, I think we would have died of fear and terror."

After the vision, the Virgin Mary said to the children, "You have seen Hell where the souls of poor sinners go. To save them, God wishes to establish in the world devotion to my Immaculate Heart. If what I say to you is done, many souls will be saved and there will be peace." She then told them, "When you pray the rosary, say after each mystery:

'O my Jesus, forgive us our sins, save us from the fire of Hell. Lead all souls to Heaven, especially those in most need of your mercy.' "

Q. During that appearance, didn't our Lady also predict the end of World War I, the coming of World War II, and the rise of Communism?

A. Yes. According to Lucia, Mary said that World War I, then in its fourth year, would end, but warned that "if people do not cease offending God, a worse one will break out during the pontificate of Pius XI [whose reign wouldn't begin until 1922 and would last until 1939]. When you see a night illumined by an unknown light, know that this is the great sign given you by God that He is about to punish the world for its crimes by means of war, famine, and persecutions of the Church and of the Holy Father."

On the night of January 25, 1938, from 9 p.m. until 2 a.m., the skies over Europe were illuminated by an unknown light that was so bright people thought whole cities were on fire. A headline in the January 26th *New York Times* read: "Aurora Borealis Startles Europe. People Flee in Fear, Call Firemen." Just a few months later, Hitler invaded Austria and World War II began.

To prevent war, famine, and persecutions, the Blessed Mother continued: "I shall come to ask for the consecration of Russia to my Immaculate Heart, and the Communion of reparation on the First Saturdays. If my requests are heeded, Russia will be converted, and there will be peace. If not, she will spread her errors throughout the world, causing wars and persecutions of the Church. The good will be martyred; the Holy Father will have much to suffer; various nations will be annihilated. In the end, my Immaculate Heart will triumph. The Holy Father will consecrate Russia to me, and she shall be converted, and a period of peace will be granted to the world."

Q. The first two secrets revealed by Sister Lucia were the vision of Hell and devotion to the Immaculate Heart and the First Saturday devotions. What was the famous Third Secret?

A. Lucia wrote down the Third Secret in 1944 and sent it to Pope Pius XII to be opened in 1960. This secret, which had long been the subject of apocalyptic speculation, was read by Pope John XXIII and by Pope Paul VI, but neither one chose to make it public. It was not revealed until June 26, 2000, when Pope John Paul II said that it referred to the assassination attempt against him on May 13, 1981, the anniversary of the Blessed Mother's first appearance to the Fatima visionaries in 1917. Here is the text of the secret:

> "We saw an angel with a flaming sword in his left hand; flashing, it gave out flames that looked as though they would set the world on fire; but they died out in contact with the splendor that our Lady radiated toward him from her right hand. Pointing to earth with his right hand, the angel cried out in a loud voice: *'Penance, Penance, Penance!'* And we saw an immense light that is God: 'something similar to how people appear in a mirror when they pass in front of it,' a Bishop dressed in white; we had the impression that it was the Holy Father.
>
> "Other Bishops, Priests, men and women Religious going up a steep mountain, at the top of which there was a big cross of rough-hewn trunks as of a cork tree with the bark; before reaching there, the Holy Father passed through a big city half in ruins and half trembling with halting step, afflicted with pain and sorrow, he prayed for the souls of the corpses he met on his way. Having reached the top of the mountain on his knees at the foot of the big cross, he was killed by a group of soldiers who fired bullets and arrows at him, and in the same way there died one after another the other Bishops, Priests,

men and women Religious, and various laypeople of different ranks and positions.

"Beneath the two arms of the cross there were two angels each with a crystal aspersorium in his hand, in which they gathered up the blood of the martyrs and with it sprinkled the souls that were making their way to God."

Q. But Pope John Paul did not die after he was shot.

A. That is true, although he was very close to death and the doctors thought that there was little hope of saving his life. The reason he was not killed, the Holy Father said later, was that "a mother's hand" had deflected the bullet away from what would have been a fatal path and "the Pope halted at the threshold of death." That bullet was subsequently set in the crown of the statue of Our Lady of Fatima in Portugal, and John Paul visited there one year after the assassination attempt to thank the Blessed Mother for saving his life.

Q. How are we to interpret the Third Secret?

A. Sister Lucia once said that "it's not my job to interpret; the interpretation is up to the Church and the Pope. I'm just telling the facts, what I saw and what I felt and perceived." So it was that Joseph Cardinal Ratzinger, realizing the need for a proper understanding of the secret, published a lengthy commentary on it in June 2000.

Among other things, Cardinal Ratzinger said that the vision shown to the children was "in no way a film preview of a future in which nothing can be changed," but "rather, the vision speaks of dangers and how we might be saved from them." He said that the scenes of a Bishop in white making his way among dead bodies through a city in ruins described the Church's *Via Crucis* [Way of the Cross], her "journey through a time of violence, destruction, and persecution. The history of an entire century can be seen represented in this image … in a compressed way. In the vision we can recognize the last century as a century of martyrs, a century of suffering and persecution for the Church, a century of world wars and the many local wars that filled the last fifty years and have inflicted unprecedented forms of cruelty."

The figure of the Pope, said Ratzinger, was "a convergence of different Popes. Beginning from Pius X up to the present Pope [John Paul II], they all shared the sufferings of the century and strove to go forward through all the anguish along the path that leads to the Cross." He said that in the death of the Bishop in white, Pope John Paul recognized the assassination attempt on him in 1981, but attributed his survival to the intervention of the Blessed Mother, proving, said Ratzinger, that "faith and prayer are forces that can influence history and that in the end prayer is more powerful than bullets and faith more powerful than armies."

The future Pope Benedict concluded by saying that the events depicted in the vision "belong to the past. Those who expected exciting apocalyptic revelations about the end of the world or the future course of history are bound to be disappointed. Fatima does not satisfy our curiosity in this way." What is important about the Third Secret, he said, is "the exhortation to prayer as the path of 'salvation for souls' and, likewise, the summons to penance and conversion."

Reflecting on our Lady's promise that "my Immaculate Heart will triumph," Ratzinger said that "the Evil One has power in this world, as we see and experience continually; he has power because our freedom continually lets us be led away from God. But since God Himself took a human heart and has thus steered human freedom toward what is good, the freedom to choose evil no longer has the last word. From that time forth, the word that prevails is this: 'In the world you will have tribulation, but take heart; I have overcome the world' (Jn 16:33). The message of Fatima invites us to trust in this promise."

Q. What do you know about a bestselling work of fiction entitled *The Third Secret*?

A. A novel that was published in 2005, *The Third Secret* followed in the wake of *The Da Vinci Code* in building a thriller around murder, intrigue, and hidden secrets in the Catholic Church. The author, Steve Berry, said that the book "grew out of my early Catholic education and a lifelong fascination with Fatima."

As is usually the case these days, the Catholic characters in the book are anything but admirable. One Pope commits suicide, his successor is a murderer, and the priest-protagonist in the story is having an affair. But the plot line is that the Church has been covering up the real Third Secret of Fatima at least since 1960.

Pope John Paul II's revelation in 2000 that the secret involved the assassination attempt on him on May 13, 1981 is not the whole story, according to the book. What the Blessed Mother really said at Fatima, Berry contends, was that abortion and homosexual relationships are okay, and that God wants women priests and married priests.

In his writer's note, the author said that "the Catholic Church is unique among man's institutions. It has not only survived for more than two millennia, but continues to grow and prosper. Yet many wonder what will be its fate in the coming century." Mr. Berry need not worry. The Catholic Church will survive until the end of the world because it was not instituted by man, but by God, who promised that His Church would last forever and that she would continue to teach the same truths that she has taught for two thousand years, including the grave moral evil of abortion and homosexual behavior, and the restriction of the priesthood to celibate men.

Q. What are the conditions for fulfilling the First Saturday devotions urged by the Blessed Mother?

A. In her appearance to the three children at Fatima on July 13th, the Blessed Mother asked for a "Communion of reparation on the First Saturdays" to bring about the conversion of Russia and world peace. She appeared again to Sister Lucia on December 10, 1925, with the Child Jesus at her side, and explained the conditions:

> "I promise to assist at the hour of death, with all the graces necessary for salvation, all those who, on the first Saturday of five consecutive months, go to Confession and receive Holy Communion, recite five decades of the rosary, and keep me company for a quarter of an hour while meditating on the mysteries of the rosary with the intention of making reparation to me."

The reason for *five* first Saturdays, rather than, say, nine, was explained by our Lord Himself when He appeared to Sister Lucia on the night of May 29-30, 1930:

> "There are five kinds of offenses and blasphemies uttered against the Immaculate Heart of Mary: (1) Blasphemies against the Immaculate Conception. (2) Blasphemies against her virginity. (3) Blasphemies against her divine maternity and at the same time refusal to recognize her as mother of men. (4) Blasphemies of those who openly seek to foster in the hearts of children indifference or contempt and even hatred for this Immaculate Mother. (5) The offenses of those who directly outrage her in her holy images."

Q. During one of the Fatima appearances, Sister Lucia asked the Blessed Virgin whether a friend who had died at the age of 18 or 19 was in Heaven. Our Lady replied, "She will be in Purgatory until the end of the world." Can that be true?

A. The statement attributed to the Blessed Mother is accurate, but we don't know what sins Lucia's friend Amelia had committed, only that she obviously had them forgiven before she died (or she wouldn't be in Purgatory), but had not done enough to make up for the temporal punishment due to them.

Every sin we commit that is forgiven, says the *Catechism* (n. 1472), "entails an unhealthy attachment to creatures, which must be purified either here on earth, or after death in the state called Purgatory. This purification frees one from what is called the 'temporal punishment' of sin." A conversion which proceeds "from a fervent charity" on earth, the *Catechism* continues, "can attain the complete purification of the sinner in such a way that no punishment would remain" [cf. Council of Trent (1551): DS 1712-1713; (1563): 1820].

Amelia's death at a young age apparently prevented her from performing the acts of fervent charity that would have eliminated or diminished the purification necessary in Purgatory. Let her fate inspire us sinners to engage in prayers, devotions, and acts of charity to make up for our own sins so that our "time" in Purgatory will be lessened, if not dispensed with altogether. One good way to accomplish this is by taking advantage of the Church's practice of indulgences, whereby we can have removed some or all of the temporal punishment due to sin by meeting the conditions set forth by the Church.

To attain a plenary indulgence, which means removal of all temporal punishment, a person must be free from all attachment to sin, even venial sin; must perform the indulgenced work as perfectly as possible; and, within several days before or after doing so, must receive sacramental Confession and Eucharistic Communion and offer prayers for the intentions of the Holy Father.

Some common indulgenced works include adoration of the Cross on Good Friday, teaching or studying Christian doctrine, attending a spiritual retreat of at least three days, reading the Bible, praying the rosary, taking part in Eucharistic adoration, making the Stations of the Cross, or visiting a parish church.

Q. What is the history of Our Lady of Guadalupe in Mexico City?

A. On December 9, 1531, a beautiful young Mexican maiden appeared to a 57-year-old Aztec Indian named Juan Diego while he was on his way to Mass. Speaking from the hill of Tepeyac, on which had once stood a pagan temple, the maiden, who seemed to be about fourteen years old, said, "Dear little son, I love you. I want you to know who I am. I am the ever-virgin Mary, Mother of the true God who gives life and maintains it in existence. He created all things. He is in all places. He is Lord of Heaven and earth."

The Lady said that she wanted a church built on that spot, and she instructed Juan to go to the Bishop in Mexico City and tell him "all that you have seen and heard." He hurried the five miles to the house of the Bishop-elect Don Fray Juan de Zumarraga and conveyed the Lady's message. Bishop Zumarraga was courteous to the Indian and said that he would give some thought to the matter.

On the way home, Juan encountered the Blessed Virgin at Tepeyac, told her that the Bishop did not seem to believe him, and suggested that she send someone "more suitable, for I am a nobody." But the Lady said that he was her messenger and he should return the next morning to the Bishop and "tell him it is the Virgin Mary who sends you."

When Juan Diego visited the Bishop the next day, Zumarraga listened patiently to his story and thought him sincere since he answered all questions without once contradicting himself. So before dismissing him, he told

Juan to ask the Virgin Mary for a sign that would confirm his story. Juan repeated the Bishop's request to Mary, and she told him to come back in the morning when she would give him a sign.

That night, however, Juan's uncle became very ill and, the next morning, hurrying to get a priest, Juan went around the other side of the hill to avoid seeing the Lady. But Mary intercepted him anyway and asked what was troubling him. The Indian explained that his uncle was dying, but Mary told him not to worry, that at that very moment his health had been restored.

She told him to go to the top of the hill, cut the flowers that were growing there, and bring them to her. Since this was December, there should not have been any flowers growing on the hill, but Juan found beautiful Castilian roses. He cut them and placed them inside his tilma or long cloak to protect them from the cold. When he returned to the Virgin Mary, she rearranged the flowers inside his tilma and sent him off to the Bishop to show him the sign and to ask him again for a church to be built there.

When Juan Diego was admitted into the presence of the Bishop, he repeated the Lady's message and then untied his tilma so Zumarraga could see the roses. Much to Juan's surprise, the Bishop and the others in the room fell to their knees for on the tilma appeared a miraculous portrait of Our Lady of Guadalupe. The Bishop had his sign, a simple chapel-like structure was built at Tepeyac, many miracles of healing were reported, and within six years, eight million natives were baptized into the Catholic Church.

Juan Diego died in 1548, but his tilma remains on display over the main altar in the Basilica of Our Lady of Guadalupe in Mexico City, and millions visit the shrine each year. He was beatified by Pope John Paul II in 1990 and raised to sainthood in 2002.

Our Lady of Guadalupe was declared patroness of Latin America in 1910 and, in 1946, Pope Pius XII declared her to be the patroness of all the Americas.

Our Lady of Guadalupe

Q. Is it true that the portrait of Our Lady of Guadalupe shows a pregnant Virgin Mary?

A. Yes, it is true. In the preface to a book entitled *A Handbook on Guadalupe*, Sean P. O'Malley, then the Bishop of Fall River, MA, and now the Archbishop of Boston, said that "it is universally believed that Mary appeared on Tepeyac Hill as the Immaculate Conception, and there is clear evidence that she is 'with child.' That is the second reason I am pleased to recommend this book which has devoted so much space to Mary as the patroness of the Pro-Life Movement in the United States."

In one of three dozen essays in the book, Fr. Paul Marx, founder of Human Life International, said that "of all the many manifestations of Mary's loving presence among us throughout the centuries, in this apparition alone does she appear to us in the manner of a pregnant mother. She holds within her the unborn Christ, proclaiming the sanctity and blessedness of life within the womb. Her reverence and tenderness communicate to us the joy and awe with which we must approach each nascent life" (p. 147).

In another essay, Dr. Janet Barber, I.H.M., an authority on Guadalupe who has been devoted to the apparition since 1952, said that in the miraculous image portrayed on Juan Diego's cloak, "her pregnancy is recognized by the high position of her sash, from the slight swelling of her abdomen most visible to the right of the sash, and the four-petaled flower over her womb .... This unique flower is the Flower of the Sun, the Nahuatl symbol Nahui Ollin, which announced to the conquered Indians that the Sun of the New Era was about to be born liturgically and in their lives, that is, the great Sun of Justice announced in Malachi [3:20], the last book of the Old Testament" (p. 135).

Our Lady's image on Juan Diego's cloak had a profound effect on the Aztec Indians, leading to the baptism of millions of them in just a few years. She had appeared as an Aztec princess and had spoken in Juan Diego's native tongue, thus associating herself with the Indians and not with their Spanish conquerors. She wore a brooch at her throat with a cross imprinted on it, showing her relationship with the God about whom the missionaries had preached. Adorned with a blue mantle covered with stars, the Virgin Mary is blocking out the sun, standing on the moon, and crushing the head of a serpent, thus telling the Indians that she is more powerful than the false gods that they had worshiped. This miraculous image gradually brought an end to child sacrifice and the beginning of worship of the one, true God. The image also showed the Spaniards that the Indians were truly human beings and were members of the Body of Christ.

Q. Didn't the Virgin Mary appear to some high school girls in Africa?

A. You are referring to Our Lady of Kibeho, who appeared to three young women from 1981 to 1989 at a Catholic girls' boarding school in the Rwandan village of Kibeho. The first apparition was on November 28, 1981 to Alphonsine Mumureke, 16, who said that the Lady identified herself as "the Mother of the Word." She told the girl to pray the rosary, to join the Legion of Mary, and to spread the faith among her schoolmates. The schoolmates, however, did not believe Alphonsine and subjected her to a merciless campaign of physical and emotional abuse.

The second visionary was Anathalie Mukamazimpaka, 17, who was told by the Virgin Mary on January 12, 1982, "You must pray, for the world is in a horrible way; people have turned from God and the love of my Son, Jesus." She warned Anathalie that if she accepted a mission of leading "lost souls back from darkness … you must also accept all the sufferings I send you with joy, love, and patience …. No one goes to Heaven without suffering." Her sufferings began immediately with the same bullying and harassment that had been inflicted on Alphonsine.

Ironically, the principal tormentor of her classmates, Marie-Claire Mukangango, had her life turned around on March 1, 1982, when the Blessed Mother appeared to her and asked her to sing Jesus' words in the Sermon on the Mount: "Blessed are you when people insult you and persecute you and falsely say all kinds of evil against you because of me."

Marie-Claire then begged for forgiveness, recanted all her accusations against her classmates, and became a model of holiness, kneeling in prayer for hours and saying the rosary. Our Lady taught her to pray the "Rosary of the Seven Sorrows," and reiterated the need for repentance.

On August 15, 1982, the Feast of the Assumption of Mary, Alphonsine was given a vision of a "river of blood," people chopping each other into pieces, and the remains of a million corpses throughout Rwanda. This was a foreshadowing of the genocide of 1994, when tribal warfare led to the horrible deaths of more than one million men, women, and children. Marie-Claire died during the slaughter while running to the aid of her husband, who was being dragged away by soldiers.

As for the other two visionaries, Alphonsine became a nun, taking the name "Alphonsine of the Glorious Cross," and Anathalie has remained in Kibeho where she carries out the Virgin Mary's request to pray and offer her suffering to bring lost souls back to God. The village was rebuilt after the 1994 genocide, and the Shrine of Our Lady of Sorrows has become a place of worship and prayer for hundreds of thousands, some of whom have claimed miraculous healings.

After twenty years of investigations, Bishop Augustin Misago declared the apparitions to the three women to be authentic. Speaking to 50,000 people at the shrine on November 28, 2001, Bishop Misago said that "Our Lady of Kibeho is a beacon of hope, a light for all of Africa and the world." For more about the history of this apparition, see the book *Our Lady of Kibeho* by Immaculee Ilibagiza, whose story of barely surviving the genocide of 1994 is told in two books, *Left to Tell* and *Led by Faith*.

Q. Isn't our Lady's appearance in the Irish village of Knock unusual in that she did not speak to the visionaries?

A. Yes, some have referred to the apparition as Our Lady of Silence. The tiny church of St. John the Baptist, whose priest had a great devotion to the souls in Purgatory, had just completed the offering of 100 Masses for the holy souls on August 21, 1879, when the apparition occurred. It was a rainy night when two women of the parish – Mary McLoughlin and Margaret Beirne – noticed a brilliant light surrounding the gable wall of the church and illuminating some figures that the women thought at first were statues placed there by the pastor. But then they saw the statues moving and recognized the Blessed Virgin, who was flanked by St. Joseph on her right and St. John the Evangelist on her left.

Mrs. Beirne rushed off to tell her neighbors about the vision and, before long, eighteen people had gathered outside the church. Ranging in age from six to seventy-five, fourteen of them would testify before a diocesan commission about what they had seen.

They said that the three figures wore dazzling white garments, that there was a brilliant crown on the Blessed Mother's head and a beautiful golden rose where the crown met her forehead, that her hands were held apart and extended upward, and that her feet were bare. St. Joseph's head was bowed toward Mary, and St. John was wearing a bishop's miter and holding a large open book in his left hand while the fingers of his right hand were raised as though preaching. Behind the trio was an altar with a lamb standing in front of a large cross. Though it was raining heavily, the ground where the people were standing was perfectly dry.

The reports of the apparition quickly spread throughout

the region and throughout Ireland and, within months, there were reports of many miracles involving cures of blindness, deafness, paralysis, epilepsy, cancer, heart trouble, bone disease, and tuberculosis. One elderly man with a grotesque growth from his neck down to his chest barely had the strength to travel to Knock, but went home strong and well after the growth had completely vanished.

In a booklet entitled *The Secret of Knock,* Rev. Dr. M. O'Carroll, CSSp, wrote:

> "The first lesson of the Apparition is the Mass. Everything seems to point to that – the altar with the sacrificial Lamb, the gesture of Our Lady, the presence of St. John in vestments, and the respectful attitude of St. Joseph .... But we may also see in the vision a reminder of another great truth connected with the Mass – the necessity of Mary's mediation and intercession and the unique character which the latter acquires because of Mary's glorious Assumption and Coronation .... No word was spoken, no oral message delivered. The Apparition does not bear in popular devotion a name or phrase giving a clue to its doctrinal meaning. Rather does it invite scrutiny, meditation, and a kind of holy wonder .... It brings us near to God."

Q. What transpired during our Lady's apparition at La Salette in France in 1846?

A. During her appearance on September 19, 1846, to two shepherd children, 14-year-old Melanie Mathieu and 11-year-old Maximin Giraud, the Blessed Virgin said that the two things most distressing to her were neglect of the Sunday Mass obligation and the misuse of her Son's name.

If people did not stop committing those sins, she said, "I shall be compelled to loose my Son's arm. It is so heavy, so pressing that I can no longer restrain it. How long I have suffered for you! If my Son is not to cast you off, I am obliged to entreat Him without ceasing. But you take no least notice of that. No matter how well you pray in the future, no matter how well you act, you will never be able to make up to me what I have endured for your sake."

Our Lady also revealed a secret to each of the children. The information was later passed on to the Pope at that time (Blessed Pope Pius IX), but the content of the secrets has never been made public.

After an investigation that lasted five years, the Bishop of the region, on November 16, 1851, ordered that the following statement be read at every Mass in his diocese:

> "We give judgment that the apparition of the Blessed Virgin to two herders on September 19, 1846, on the mountain of the Alpine chain situated in the parish of La Salette, in the territory of the archpriest of Corps, bears in itself all the marks of truth, and the faithful have grounds to believe it indubitable and certain."

Q. What do you know about the Blessed Virgin's many appearances to a woman in the French village of Laus between 1664 and 1718?

A. The woman's name was Benoite (Benedicta) Rencurel, and she was only seventeen when our Lady first appeared daily to her over a period of four months. She told the young woman that "my name is Mary" and instructed her to "pray continuously for sinners." When a woman secretly followed Benoite to the site of the apparitions, the Blessed Mother told Benoite to warn the woman that her soul was in danger. "She has something on her conscience," Mary said. "Tell her to do penance." Moved by the warning, the woman turned away from her sins and lived a holy life.

During her many appearances, the Virgin Mary asked Benoite to admonish women and girls to live chaste lives and not to have abortions. She warned against acquiring wealth unjustly, and encouraged priests and religious to be faithful to their vows. Our Lady also told the seer to construct a small church there and promised that the oil from the sanctuary lamp would work miracles for the sick if they received anointing with faith in her intercession.

Between 1669 and 1679, Benedicta received five visions of the suffering Christ, who told her, "My daughter, I show myself in this state so that you can participate in my Passion." She suffered greatly during the final two decades of her life, while receiving consolation from the Virgin Mary, and died on December 28, 1718.

On May 4, 2008, Archbishop Georges Pontier of Marseille announced a decree recognizing the "supernatural origin of the apparitions and of facts lived and recounted by the young shepherdess." He said that "three centuries have passed since Benoite Rencurel testified about what Christ and Mary, His mother, had revealed concerning God's love for men, as well as His infinite mercy and His appeal for conversion."

Pontier said that "here, as in Lourdes, as in La Salette, as in Fatima, we see Mary pursuing her mission to reveal her Son and invite us to do as He tells us .... The greatness of Benoite lies not in her intellectual capacities, her diplomas, or her fortune, or the style of her social circle, but the fact that she agreed to be chosen by the Lord to reveal the tenderness of God through Mary. She invites everyone in a very personal way to conversion."

Q. What about our Lady's appearance to Catherine Laboure and the origin of the Miraculous Medal?

A. Catherine Laboure was nine years old when her mother died in 1815, and one day in the midst of her grief she climbed on a chair and took down a statue of the Virgin Mary that was on a high shelf in her mother's bedroom. "Now, dear Blessed Mother," Catherine said, "you will be my mother." Little did she know how true that would be.

At the age of 23, Catherine entered the convent of the Sisters of Charity at 140 Rue du Bac in Paris. On the night of July 18, 1830, a young child dressed in white woke her and said, "Come to the chapel, the Blessed Virgin is waiting for you there." Mary was indeed in the chapel and she engaged the young woman in conversation for two hours.

Among other things, the beautiful Lady told Catherine that "you will have much to suffer, but you will rise above these sufferings by reflecting that what you do is for the glory of God .... Have confidence. Do not be afraid." She said that "the times are very evil. Sorrows will befall France; the throne will be overturned. The whole world will be plunged into every kind of misery. But come to the foot of the altar. There graces will be shed upon all, great and small, who ask for them."

Her predictions that "the cross will be treated with contempt ... the streets will run with blood," and the archbishop will be struck down came true during the revolutions of 1830, 1848, and 1870. Archbishop Affre was shot to death in 1848, and Archbishop Darboy was murdered in 1870.

The most memorable of the Virgin Mary's appearances occurred on November 27, 1830, when she told Catherine to have a religious medal struck in her honor. The front of the medal was to show the Blessed Mother standing on a globe that represented the world, with an inscription around the top and sides of the medal that said, "O Mary, conceived without sin, pray for us who have recourse to thee."

On the back there was to be a large M surmounted by a bar and a cross and below the M the Hearts of Jesus and Mary, one crowned with thorns, the other pierced with a sword. There were also twelve stars around the oval, recalling Revelation 12:1, which describes "a woman clothed with the sun, with the moon under her feet, and on her head a crown of twelve stars."

At first, the medal was known as the Medal of the Immaculate Conception, but after the spread of the medal led to many reported cures and favors through the intercession of Mary, it became known as the Miraculous Medal. Millions of people have worn this medal since 1830, and it has led to conversions, repentance of hardened sinners, peace in families, and recoveries from a variety of illnesses. The Blessed Virgin has kept her promise that those who wear the medal around their neck "will receive great graces."

Catherine Laboure died on December 31, 1876 and was raised to sainthood by Pope Pius XII in 1947. Her incorrupt body lies beneath an altar on the spot where her second Mother first appeared to her.

Q. What is the background of the famous shrine to Our Lady at Lourdes in France?

A. From February 11 to July 16, 1858, the Blessed Mother appeared eighteen times to a very poor and sickly 14-year-old peasant girl named Bernadette Soubirous. At the ninth apparition on February 25th, the 350 people present saw Bernadette kiss the ground, poke a hole in the earth and smear her face with mud, drink the water bubbling out of the ground, and eat a few weeds growing near the grotto. When people asked her why she had done that, Bernadette said that the Lady wanted her to offer up her humiliation for sinners, and besides, she said, "We eat salad, don't we?"

With 1,500 people present on March 1st, a woman from the village, whose fingers had been paralyzed in a fall from a tree, dragged her two little children to the pool that had formed and bathed her hand in the water. To her astonishment, the paralysis went away and her fingers were healed. This was the first of many miracles at Lourdes.

Despite taunts by other children and interrogations by local officials, Bernadette never wavered in her reports of her encounters with the Virgin Mary. She gave this description of her heavenly visitor:

Our Lady of Lourdes

"She has the appearance of a young girl of sixteen or seventeen. She is dressed in a white robe, girdled at the waist with a blue ribbon which flows down all around it. A yoke closes it in graceful pleats at the base of the neck; the sleeves are long and tight-fitting. She wears upon her head a veil which is also white; this veil gives just a glimpse of her hair and then falls down at the back below her waist. Her feet are bare but covered by the last folds of her robe, except at the point where a yellow rose shines upon each of them. She holds on her right arm a rosary of white beads with a chain of gold shining like the two roses on her feet."

As in appearances by our Lady in other lands, she told Bernadette to "pray for sinners," and later stressed the threefold warning of "Penitence, Penitence, Penitence!" But the most convincing proof that the apparitions were genuine came on the Feast of the Annunciation, March 25, 1858, when the Virgin Mary said, "I am the Immaculate Conception."

There was no way that Bernadette could have known the meaning of our Lady's words, but when she reported them to her priest, he was stunned because, just four years earlier, Pope Pius IX had proclaimed to the whole world the dogma of the Immaculate Conception, which holds that the Blessed Virgin Mary was free from Original Sin from the moment of her conception in her mother's womb.

Four years after Bernadette had her last vision of the Blessed Mother, and prayed the rosary with her, Bishop Bertrand-Severe Laurence declared that seven of the healings in the Lourdes water were miracles, and he solemnly proclaimed: "It is our judgment that the Immaculate Mother of God has truly appeared to Bernadette."

Bernadette left Lourdes in 1866, entered a convent hundreds of miles away, and took the name Sister Marie-Bernard. She remained there until her death in 1879 at the age of 35. She devoted her life to prayer and never complained about the mean treatment she received from the Mother Superior of the convent, who couldn't understand why the Holy Virgin would appear to an illiterate peasant girl and not to a well-educated nun. After she died, friends remembered what the Virgin Mary had said to Bernadette in one of her appearances: "I do not promise to make you happy in this world, but in the next." She was declared a saint in 1933.

Meanwhile, a chapel had been built at the grotto and then expanded into a basilica, baths were constructed so that the sick could bathe in them, and what began as a trickle of water now flows at the rate of 32,000 gallons a day. Millions of visitors come to Lourdes each year, 70,000 of them sick and dying and seeking the healing touch of Mary and her Son. There have been more than 5,000 reported cures at Lourdes since 1858, but the Church has recognized less than 70 of them as miracles. Some examples:

A man whose leg was broken and there was a space between the bones that would not heal. It became infected and doctors wanted to cut off his leg. But when he put his leg in the water at Lourdes, it was instantly healed. New bone had grown in the open space. A 24-year-old woman who weighed 55 pounds and was dying was brought to Lourdes and placed on a stretcher in front of the grotto. As a Eucharistic procession went by her, with the priest holding up the Blessed Sacrament for all to adore, the woman was hurled from her stretcher and fell on her knees. A moment later, she stood up and began to walk, shouting, "I am healed." Over the next few months, she gained 77 pounds and resumed a normal life that was devoted to caring for the sick.

Apart from the miracles, there are two other impressive things about Lourdes. First, many of those who are not cured of physical problems are cured emotionally and spiritually. In other words, their minds and souls are healed so that they are able to cope with their disability.

Second, there has been at Lourdes since 1882 a Medical Bureau that is run by doctors for doctors. Every year, thousands of medical specialists come to Lourdes to study the cures. They are persons of all religions and of no religion. They speak from a scientific perspective, not a religious point of view. The procedure followed at Lourdes is worth studying.

No sick person is accepted there without a medical certificate from his or her own doctor, stating the nature and present condition of the disease. When an alleged cure takes place, the patient is immediately examined by the doctors who are registered at the Medical Bureau. They are interested in three things: (1) Did the disease really exist? (2) Can it be cured? (3) Is there a natural explanation for the cure?

If the doctors feel that there might have been a cure, they send the patient home, put him under the observation of a physician, and invite him to come back in a year. The second examination is much more rigorous than the first one because the doctors will be risking their professional reputations when they either sign or refuse to sign the final report. But if the doctors believe that a cure has taken place, they send the patient's complete medical record to the International Medical Committee of Lourdes in Paris. After its own thorough investigation of the case, that committee issues its judgment that there is no medical or scientific explanation for the cure.

The case is then forwarded to the bishop of the person's diocese, whose task is to determine if the cure meets the following conditions: (1) The disease must have been serious and virtually impossible to cure. (2) No medication was used or, if it was, it had no effect on the disease. (3) The cure must have been instantaneous and perfect. (4) The disease must never appear again.

If all these conditions are fulfilled, then the bishop will declare that a miracle has taken place. For an account of 150 miraculous stories that took place in Lourdes between 1858 and 2008, see the book *The Wonders of Lourdes*.

Q. What do you know about Our Lady of the Pillar in Saragossa, Spain?

A. According to an ancient tradition, the Blessed Virgin appeared to St. James the Apostle while he was praying near Saragossa around the year A.D. 40 and encouraged him and seven of his disciples to build a chapel there. The Virgin left them a column made of jasper upon which stood a small statue of her. The chapel built over the spot of the apparition was eventually destroyed, as were several replacements, but the 15-inch-high statue atop the six-foot-tall pillar can be seen today in the Church of the Virgin of the Pillar in Saragossa. This seventeenth-century church was declared a national museum in 1905 and is visited by thousands of pilgrims each year. Pope John Paul II stopped at this ancient shrine during a tour of Spain in 1982.

Q. Wasn't one of the the earliest recorded apparitions of the Blessed Virgin in Walsingham, England, in 1061.

A. Tradition indicates that the Blessed Mother appeared in 1061 to a holy Saxon woman, Richeldis de Faverches, took her in spirit to our Lady's home in Nazareth, and commanded her to build a duplicate of that home in Walsingham. The holy house was built, a spring of water miraculously appeared nearby, and the shrine became a place of pilgrimage and of many miraculous cures.

King Henry VIII was reportedly a devotee of the shrine while he was a Catholic, but had it destroyed during the Reformation in the sixteenth century. The shrine was revived early in the twentieth century after a statue of the Blessed Virgin and the Christ Child was carved and later placed in a house that was built as near as possible to the dimensions of the first house in Walsingham.

Pope Leo XIII (1878-1903) had commissioned a statue of Our Lady of Walsingham and had it sent to the shrine and, when Pope John Paul II visited Wembley Stadium in England in 1982, he requested that the statue be brought from Walsingham for his Mass. At the request of the Catholic Bishops of England and Wales, the Vatican in 2001 established the Feast of Our Lady of Walsingham to be celebrated each year on September 24th.

Q. Have there been any approved Marian apparitions in the United States?

A. Yes. On December 8, 2010, Bishop David L. Ricken of Green Bay, Wisconsin, announced approval of three apparitions of the Blessed Mother to Adele Brise in October 1859 about eighteen miles northeast of Green Bay. The official decree came nearly two years after Bishop Ricken appointed three theologians, all internationally recognized experts in the theology of the Virgin Mary, to study the history of the reported appearances.

Brise, a 28-year-old immigrant from Belgium, was walking home October 9th from Sunday Mass in Bay Settlement, about eleven miles from her house, when our Lady appeared to her for the third time. When Brise asked who she was, Mary replied, "I am the Queen of Heaven who prays for the conversion of all sinners, and I wish you to do the same."

The Blessed Virgin told Brise to "gather the children in this wild country and teach them what they should know for salvation. Teach them their catechism, how to sign themselves with the Sign of the Cross, and how to approach the Sacraments." After her father built a small chapel near the spot of the apparitions, Brise began a community of Third Order Franciscan sisters, built a school next to the chapel, and devoted the rest of her life to teaching children. She died in 1896.

The current chapel at the site was dedicated in 1942 under the title of Our Lady of Good Help, and thousands of visitors come to the shrine each year.

Disapproved Apparitions

Q. What is the Army of Mary?

A. The Army of Mary was founded in Quebec in 1971 by Marie-Paul Giguere, who said that she was receiving visions from God. According to the group's publications, Giguere claimed to be the reincarnation of the Blessed Virgin, a claim that led Church authorities in Canada in 1987 to warn that the Army of Mary could not be considered Catholic.

After the organization performed what it called ordinations in 2007, Marc Cardinal Ouellet of Quebec declared that the priest who conducted the ordination ceremony had no authority to do so and, shortly thereafter, the Vatican's Sacred Congregation for the Doctrine of the Faith excommunicated certain members of the Army for performing ordinations without Church permission.

Q. What about the alleged apparitions of the Blessed Virgin in Bayside, New York?

A. In a pamphlet entitled "Bayside: The Facts Revealed," which was published by the St. Michael's World Apostolate, it says that "there has never been a true, thorough, canonical investigation of Bayside," that the "whole so-called 'investigation' " conducted by the Diocese of Brooklyn was "a gross abuse of power," and that in the 1986 letter from then-Bishop Francis Mugavero, warning that the alleged messages from the Blessed Virgin were contrary to Catholic teaching, "not one example is given. And this from a bishop whose primary duty is to teach!"

Devotees of Bayside believe that the Virgin Mary appeared more than 300 times, from 1970 to 1995, to a woman named Veronica Lueken, who died in 1995. Bishop Mugavero said in 1986 that "no credibility can be given to the so-called 'apparitions' reported by Veronica Lueken and her followers." The bishop said that "the 'messages' and other related propaganda contain statements which, among other things, are contrary to the teachings of the Catholic Church, undermine the legitimate authority of bishops and councils, and instill doubts in the minds of the faithful, for example, by claiming that, for years, an 'imposter Pope' governed the Catholic Church in the place of Paul VI."

Let's look at that last claim before getting into the doctrinal errors contained in the alleged messages. Bayside supporters at one time distributed a 40-page tabloid-sized newspaper containing more than 120 photographs of Pope Paul and his alleged imposter. The tabloid attempted to prove that they were two different men by pointing out differences in the size and the shape of the Pontiff's nose and ears.

The pictures were taken over a period of 15 years, and they were taken from different angles and in different lighting, which surely explains why the Holy Father didn't always look exactly the same. But only someone with a preconceived notion could look at those photos and come to the conclusion that they were of two different men.

Furthermore, there were many statements attributed to the Blessed Mother by Mrs. Lueken that only the credulous could ever believe had come from our Lady. For example, Mary was reported to have said in 1973 that the late Jesuit paleontologist Teilhard de Chardin "is in Hell," in 1976 that Freemasonry is "a synagogue of Satan," in 1977 that "Satan has full control" of the Church, in 1981 that altar railings should be restored in Catholic churches, and in 1985 that "Jesus wishes that the Old Mass be returned to wipe out many of the errors that have crept in since the New Mass has started."

In 1993, Bishop Mugavero's successor, Bishop Thomas Daily, who had endorsed his predecessor's negative judgment on the Bayside events, was asked again for his comments. His chancellor, Msgr. Otto Garcia, sent out an information packet on Bayside that spelled out some of the doctrinal errors contained in statements attributed to the Virgin Mary. Here are a few of them:

Item: The Blessed Virgin is reported to have said on June 18, 1986: "My children, but I, as your Mother, must treat you at this time as adults, being able to reason with the God-given reasoning that Heaven gave unto you when you were conceived by the Holy Ghost."

Comment: Only Jesus was conceived by the Holy Ghost. All other human beings were conceived in the normal human fashion.

Item: On August 14, 1979, the Blessed Mother was quoted as saying: "Do not judge your brothers and sisters who have not been converted. For my Father's house, my Son has repeated over and over, remember always that my Father's house – there are many rooms in the mansion, signifying faith and creeds. However, the Eternal Father, the Beatific Vision, is reserved for the Roman Catholic following. This – it has been deemed by the Eternal Father since the beginning of time."

Comment: The idea that in Heaven there will be certain rooms for those of other faiths and creeds, and a special room for Catholics, is not a part of Church teaching.

Item: On May 30, 1978, the Blessed Mother is reported to have said: "The Church of my Son, that is being stripped of all holiness, shall emerge with the world and with the world's leaders to be directed for a short time by Satan."

Comment: To suggest that at some point in time, Satan will direct the Church of Christ is to contradict two explicit promises of our Lord, namely, that the gates of Hell will never prevail against His Church (cf. Matthew 16:18) and that He will be with His Church "always, until the end of the age" (Matthew 28:20).

Refusing to believe that our Lady could ever have said such absurd things does not show "deep-seated prejudice" or "astonishing ignorance," as Bayside supporters contend. It shows common sense. You won't find statements like these in the approved apparitions of the Virgin Mary at Guadalupe, La Salette, Lourdes, and Fatima.

There is no doubt that there are many believers in Bayside who are sincere and well-meaning people. But they will have to concede the same sincerity and good will to those who have looked at the facts about Bayside and don't believe that the Blessed Mother appeared there from 1970 to 1995.

They will also have to pardon those who don't contact the St. Michael World Apostolate "for the Message from Heaven, including a free rose petal blessed by Jesus and Mary with the power of cure and conversion."

Q. What about making pilgrimages to an alleged apparition site in Conyers, Georgia?

A. On March 9, 1992, Archbishop James P. Lyke, now deceased, declared that "the authenticity of these alleged apparitions is in grave doubt." His successor as Archbishop of Atlanta, John F. Donoghue, later expressed his agreement with the conclusion of Archbishop Lyke.

Q. What do you know about alleged visions to a Theresa Lopez in Denver, Colorado?

A. After an investigation that took over two years, then-Archbishop of Denver J. Francis Stafford issued the following statement in 1994:

> "On December 9, 1991, I appointed a commission to investigate alleged apparitions of the Blessed Virgin Mary at Mother Cabrini Shrine and other places within the Archdiocese of Denver to Theresa Antonia Lopez. On February 22, 1994, the commission completed its investigation and presented its findings to me.
>
> "As Archbishop of Denver, I have concluded that the alleged apparitions of the Blessed Virgin Mary to Theresa Antonia Lopez are devoid of any supernatural origin. Because of my concern for the spiritual welfare of the People of God, I direct the faithful to refrain from participating in or promoting paraliturgical or liturgical services related to the alleged apparitions.
>
> "Furthermore, anyone encouraging devotion to these alleged apparitions in any way is acting contrary to my wishes as Archbishop of Denver. It remains my constant

hope that all the faithful will promote devotions to our Blessed Lady in the many forms which have been approved by the Catholic Church."

Q. Is there any reason to believe the claims of a woman in Emmitsburg, Maryland, that the Blessed Virgin had told her of a worldwide disaster that will result in the deaths of 60 to 70 percent of the world's population?

A. No, there is no reason to believe the claims made by Gianna Talone-Sullivan, who said that the Virgin Mary conveyed messages to her during Thursday evening prayer services at St. Joseph's Church in Emmitsburg from 1993 to 2000. Following an "extensive study by a commission comprised of experts in the fields of theology and canon law," William Cardinal Keeler, then the Archbishop of Baltimore, issued a statement on August 29, 2008, that said the alleged visions were not supernatural.

"The commission's finding," said the Archdiocesan statement, "was based in part on the fact that many of the messages were apocalyptic in nature, placed undue emphasis on future destruction, and called for great and miraculous signs – all of which are incompatible with [the] tradition and teachings of the Catholic Church."

The decree of Cardinal Keeler was approved by Joseph Cardinal Ratzinger, then the Prefect of the Congregation for the Doctrine of the Faith and now Pope Benedict XVI. A few months later, Cardinal Keeler's successor, Archbishop Edwin O'Brien, ordered Mrs. Talone-Sullivan not to communicate with others about her alleged apparitions. In an advisory to area parishes, O'Brien wrote:

> "I strongly caution Mrs. Gianna Talone-Sullivan not to communicate in any manner – written or spoken, electronic or printed, personally or through another in any church or any other place, public or private, within the jurisdiction of the Archdiocese of Baltimore

– any information of any type related to or containing messages or locutions allegedly received from the Virgin Mother of God. It is my hope that this warning will result in greater clarity for the faithful and resolve the divisions created by this situation."

Mrs. Talone-Sullivan said that she would abide by the archbishop's order and cancel all public appearances.

Q. What do you know about a woman in England who said that the Blessed Mother had told her that the Church must proclaim aborted babies to be martyrs?

A. The woman's name is Patricia De Menezes, she lives in a suburb of London, and she founded the Community of Divine Innocence to promote "holiness and innocence within God's family." In 2007, however, the Archbishop of the diocese in which she lives, Most Rev. Kevin McDonald of Southwark, released a letter from the Vatican's Sacred Congregation for the Doctrine of the Faith, which said that Mrs. De Menezes' claims were exaggerated and doctrinally problematic.

"Given that the supposed revelations which ground the spirituality of the Community are highly questionable," said Archbishop Angelo Amata of the Vatican Congregation, "it follows that the community's spirituality is flawed at its root. Because this spirituality thoroughly animates the community's proposed constitution, it cannot be approved."

Archbishop Amato specifically rejected Mrs. De Menezes' statement about the martyrdom of all the innocent children deliberately killed before birth. He said that "a martyr is someone who bears witness to Christ. If the victims of abortion were to qualify for martyrdom, it would then seem that all victims of any moral evil should likewise be deemed martyrs."

In his own statement, Archbishop McDonald said the ruling means that there is "no ecclesiastical approbation for Catholics to meet as the group known as Divine Innocence.

I am aware that many devout people, deeply committed to the Pro-Life movement, have become involved with Divine Innocence. I wish to encourage them in their work and prayer, but in view of the observations of the Congregation for the Doctrine of the Faith, this must no longer be in the context of the organization or spirituality of the Divine Innocence."

Q. What about the alleged visions of the Blessed Virgin Mary in Necedah, Wisconsin, in the 1950s?

A. Mary Ann Van Hoof, who died in 1984, began claiming in the 1950s that the Blessed Mother was appearing to her in Necedah. People soon flocked to the site, but the Bishop of La Crosse, the diocese in which Necedah is located, concluded after a five-year investigation that the claims of Mrs. Van Hoof were false.

Another bishop of that diocese came to the same conclusion in 1969 and, in 1975, the bishop placed the leaders of the shrine under personal interdict, which meant that they could not receive the Sacraments. When in 1979 Mrs. Van Hoof and her followers brought in a phony "archbishop" to consecrate the shrine, the Bishop of La Crosse issued a statement that said, among other things:

> "For the guidance of the faithful, it should be noted that this action on the part of Mrs. Mary Ann Van Hoof and her followers joined in 'For My God and Country Inc.' definitely establishes that they are no longer affiliated with the Roman Catholic Church and acknowledge this separation by this action of approving the celebration of the Holy Sacrifice of the Mass by an unauthorized person."

Unapproved Apparitions

Q. What do we know about the reported appearances of our Lady in Akita, Japan in 1973?

A. According to the latest information we have, two Japanese bishops have not definitively confirmed that the Blessed Virgin appeared three times in 1973 to Sister Agnes Sasagawa, but neither have they declared that nothing supernatural occurred in the Japanese village of Akita. Here is a statement issued on August 18, 1993, by the Most Reverend Franciscus Keiichi Sato, O.F.M., the bishop of Niigata, Japan:

> "1. Even today opinions differ about whether the statue of Our Lady at Yuzawadai, Akita (the statue which shed tears) should be venerated or not. While pilgrims continue to increase, there are also many priests who are against it.
>
> "2. The fact that the wooden statue of Our Lady shed tears is undeniable. It is something that occurred over and over (101 times) between 1975 and 1981, with a great number of eyewitnesses.
>
> "3. The first investigating commission, set up at the request of Bishop [John Shojiro] Ito (Ordinary of Niigata at the time), found that 'the supernatural nature of the events cannot be proved.' Bishop Ito, however, was not satisfied with this conclusion and, after consulting with Rome, established a second investigating commission.
>
> "4. The findings of the second investigating commission were reported in 1984 in a pastoral letter of Bishop Ito: 'It is not possible to make a negative statement that there is no supernaturality. Also, nothing can be found that is opposed to faith or morals. Consequently, until a final judgment is handed down by the Holy See, I will not forbid the showing of veneration within this diocese towards the holy statue of Akita.'
>
> "5. In 1985, Bishop Ito resigned and I, Bishop Sato, succeeded him. I have not passed any subsequent judgment, and therefore the report of Bishop Ito is still valid.
>
> "6. At present, Yuzawadai in Akita appears to be

taking hold as a place of prayer. It cannot be compared with Lourdes or Fatima, but it definitely has an atmosphere of prayer, and many pilgrims visit both from within the country and from overseas.

"7. I believe that time will clarify whether this is a work of God or of human beings. In [the] future, it is my intention to neither especially encourage veneration and pilgrimages to the aforesaid statue of Our Lady, nor to forbid them."

Q. What is the Church's position on the alleged visions of our Blessed Mother at Garabandal in Spain?

A. After reports that our Lady had appeared to a group of four girls, ages eleven and twelve, in that town in northern Spain from 1961 to 1965, Bishop Vicente Montis, the Ordinary of the diocese where Garabandal is located, conducted an investigation and declared that "there have been no apparitions of the Blessed Virgin, of Michael the Archangel, or of any other celestial person; there have been no messages. All of the reported happenings in that area have a natural explanation."

That finding was upheld by Bishop Montis' successor the following year and again in 1977 by Bishop Antonio Del Val Gallo after he had met with those said to have been involved in the reported events in the early Sixties. In the mid-Eighties, Bishop Del Val opened another investigation into the matter "because I thought something serious had happened in Garabandal." He said that the results of that investigation were given in 1991 to Joseph Cardinal Ratzinger, then the prefect of the Vatican's Sacred Congregation for the Doctrine of the Faith.

In an interview that appeared in the October/December 1993 issue of *Garabandal* magazine, Del Val said that he found the messages of Garabandal to be "theologically correct, yes, but one of the details bothers me: 'Many bishops and cardinals are walking the path of perdition.' It seems to me to be a bit severe. However, the messages do not say anything that is against the doctrine of the Church."

The Bishop went on to say that "it is important for us Christians to live what the messages of the Blessed Mother are saying – but I'm not saying that she did, since this would be admitting that the apparitions are true, and I cannot do that because the Church has not yet said so. The Church is the one with the last word."

Eight years later, in a letter dated August 23, 2001, His Excellency Jose Vilaplana, who had become the Bishop of Santander in 1991, said that he had asked the Sacred Congregation for the Doctrine of the Faith for guidance. The Congregation responded to him on November 28, 1992, said Bishop Vilaplana, and said that "after having examined carefully all the documents, they did not find it necessary to intervene directly or to withdraw this affair from the ordinary jurisdiction of the Bishop of Santander, which is his by right."

He said the SCDF "suggested that if I considered it appropriate, I should publish a declaration to reiterate the fact that there is no evidence to support the supernatural nature of the alleged apparitions, and so make my own the unanimous position of my predecessors. As the statements of my predecessors who had studied the case had been clear and unanimous, I did not consider it necessary to make a new public declaration, and I wished to avoid drawing attention to matters which were now well in the past."

That is how things stand at the time this is written.

Q. Has the Church made a final determination on the reported appearances of our Lady in the Bosnian village of Medjugorje?

A. Not as of the time this book was written. In March 2010, the Vatican's Sacred Congregation for the Doctrine of the

Faith established a commission made up of "cardinals, bishops, specialists, and experts" to investigate reports that the Blessed Virgin first appeared to six children in Medjugorje in 1981 and has been appearing to some of them on a daily basis ever since. The commission was to be headed by Camillo Cardinal Ruini, a retired archbishop of Rome, and is expected to "take some time" studying the phenomenon.

Millions of pilgrims have traveled to Medjugorje since 1981, and there have been claims of miraculous physical cures and spiritual conversions. However, the local bishop has repeatedly questioned the authenticity of the apparitions and, in 1991, the Yugoslavian Bishops' Conference declared by a vote of 19 to 1: "On the basis of inquiries conducted up to the present time, one cannot affirm that we are dealing here with supernatural apparitions or revelations."

Rosa Mystica

Chapter 5

Marian Litanies

Q. What is the background for the many titles and invocations to the Blessed Virgin Mary, such as Tower of David, Tower of Ivory, House of Gold, Mystical Rose, Mirror of Justice, Seat of Wisdom, and Star of the Sea?
A. These invocations and titles are taken from the Litany of Loreto, which dates from the twelfth century and was approved for public worship in 1587 by Pope Sixtus V. They also stem from the prayers of the Greek Church, in particular the Akathist Hymn, which was translated into Latin and first published in Venice about the year 800, and they are further based on the writings of the Fathers of the first six centuries of the Church.

Here are some of the well-known litanies to our Lady.

Litany of Loreto

Lord, have mercy. Christ, have mercy.
Lord, have mercy. Christ, have mercy.
Christ, hear us. Christ, graciously hear us.
God the Father of heaven, have mercy on us.
God the Son, Redeemer of the world, have mercy on us.
God the Holy Spirit, have mercy on us.
Holy Trinity, one God, have mercy on us.
Holy Mary, pray for us.
Holy Mother of God, pray for us.
Holy Virgin of Virgins, pray for us.
Mother of Christ, pray for us.
Mother of divine grace, pray for us.
Mother most pure, pray for us.
Mother most chaste, pray for us.
Mother inviolate, pray for us.
Mother undefiled, pray for us.
Mother most amiable, pray for us.
Mother most admirable, pray for us.
Mother of good counsel, pray for us.
Mother of our Creator, pray for us.
Mother of our Savior, pray for us.

Virgin most prudent, pray for us.
Virgin most venerable, pray for us.
Virgin most renowned, pray for us.
Virgin most powerful, pray for us.
Virgin most merciful, pray for us.
Virgin most faithful, pray for us.
Mirror of justice, pray for us.
Seat of wisdom, pray for us.
Cause of our joy, pray for us.
Spiritual vessel, pray for us.
Vessel of honor, pray for us.
Singular vessel of devotion, pray for us.
Mystical Rose, pray for us.
Tower of David, pray for us.
Tower of ivory, pray for us.
House of gold, pray for us.
Ark of the Covenant, pray for us.
Gate of Heaven, pray for us.
Morning Star, pray for us.
Health of the sick, pray for us.
Refuge of sinners, pray for us.
Comforter of the afflicted, pray for us.
Help of Christians, pray for us.

Queen of angels, pray for us.
Queen of patriarchs, pray for us.
Queen of prophets, pray for us.
Queen of Apostles, pray for us.
Queen of martyrs, pray for us.
Queen of confessors, pray for us.
Queen of virgins, pray for us.
Queen of all saints, pray for us.
Queen conceived without Original Sin, pray for us.
Queen assumed into Heaven, pray for us.
Queen of the most holy rosary, pray for us.
Queen of peace, pray for us.
Lamb of God, who takes away the sins of the world,
spare us, O Lord.
Lamb of God, who takes away the sins of the world,
graciously hear us, O Lord.
Lamb of God, who takes away the sins of the world,
have mercy on us.

Pray for us, O holy Mother of God, that we may be made worthy of the promises of Christ.
Let us pray: Grant, we beseech Thee, O Lord God, that we thy servants may enjoy perpetual health of mind and body, and by the glorious intercession of Blessed Mary, ever Virgin, may we be freed from present sorrow, and rejoice in eternal happiness, through Christ our Lord. Amen.

Litany of the Blessed Virgin Mary

Lord, have mercy on us. Christ, have mercy on us.
Lord, have mercy on us. Christ, have mercy on us.
Christ, hear us. Christ, graciously hear us.
God, the Father of Heaven, have mercy on us.
God, the Son, Redeemer of the world, have mercy on us.
God, the Holy Spirit, have mercy on us.
Holy Trinity, one God, have mercy on us.
Holy Mary, pray for us.
Holy Mother of God, pray for us.
Holy Virgin of virgins, pray for us.
Mother of Christ, pray for us.
Mother of divine grace, pray for us.
Mother most pure, pray for us.
Mother most chaste, pray for us.
Mother inviolate, pray for us.
Mother undefiled, pray for us.
Mother most amiable, pray for us.
Mother most admirable, pray for us.
Mother of good counsel, pray for us.
Mother of our Creator, pray for us.
Mother of our Savior, pray for us.
Virgin most prudent, pray for us.
Virgin most venerable, pray for us.
Virgin most renowned, pray for us.
Virgin most powerful, pray for us.
Virgin most merciful, pray for us.
Virgin most faithful, pray for us.
Mirror of justice, pray for us.
Seat of wisdom, pray for us.
Cause of our joy, pray for us.
Spiritual vessel, pray for us.
Vessel of honor, pray for us.
Singular vessel of devotion, pray for us.

Mystical Rose, pray for us.
Tower of David, pray for us.
Tower of ivory, pray for us.
House of gold, pray for us.
Ark of the Covenant, pray for us.
Gate of Heaven, pray for us.
Morning Star, pray for us.
Health of the sick, pray for us.
Refuge of sinners, pray for us.
Comforter of the afflicted, pray for us.
Help of Christians, pray for us.
Queen of angels, pray for us.
Queen of patriarchs, pray for us.
Queen of prophets, pray for us.
Queen of Apostles, pray for us.
Queen of martyrs, pray for us.
Queen of confessors, pray for us.
Queen of virgins, pray for us.
Queen of all saints, pray for us.
Queen conceived without Original Sin, pray for us.
Queen assumed into Heaven, pray for us.
Queen of the most holy rosary, pray for us.
Queen of peace, pray for us.
Lamb of God, who takes away the sins of the world,
spare us, O Lord.
Lamb of God, who takes away the sins of the world,
graciously hear us, O Lord.
Lamb of God, who takes away the sins of the world,
have mercy on us.
Pray for us, O holy Mother of God, that we may be made worthy of the promises of Christ.
Let us pray: Grant, we beseech Thee, O Lord God, unto us Thy servants, that we may rejoice in continual health of mind and body; and, by the glorious intercession of Blessed Mary ever Virgin, may be delivered from present sadness and enter into the joy of thine eternal gladness, through Christ our Lord. Amen.

Litany to the Immaculate Heart of Mary

Lord, have mercy. Lord, have mercy.
Christ, have mercy. Christ, have mercy.
Lord, have mercy. Lord, have mercy.

Christ, hear us. Christ, graciously hear us.
God the Father of Heaven, have mercy on us.
God the Son, Redeemer of the world, have mercy on us.
God the Holy Spirit, have mercy on us.
Holy Trinity, one God, have mercy on us.
Heart of Mary, pray for us.
Heart of Mary, after God's own Heart, pray for us.
Heart of Mary, in union with the Heart of Jesus, pray for us.
Heart of Mary, the vessel of the Holy Spirit, pray for us.
Heart of Mary, shrine of the Trinity, pray for us.
Heart of Mary, home of the Word, pray for us.
Heart of Mary, immaculate in your creation, pray for us.
Heart of Mary, flooded with grace, pray for us.
Heart of Mary, blessed of all hearts, pray for us.
Heart of Mary, throne of glory, pray for us.
Heart of Mary, abyss of humbleness, pray for us.
Heart of Mary, victim of love, pray for us.
Heart of Mary, nailed to the cross, pray for us.
Heart of Mary, comfort of the sad, pray for us.
Heart of Mary, refuge of the sinner, pray for us.
Heart of Mary, hope of the dying, pray for us.
Heart of Mary, seat of mercy, pray for us.
Lamb of God, who takes away the sins of the world,
spare us, O Lord.
Lamb of God, who takes away the sins of the world,
graciously hear us, O Lord.
Lamb of God, who takes away the sins of the world,
have mercy on us.
Christ, hear us. Christ, graciously hear us.
Lord, have mercy. Christ, have mercy. Lord, have mercy.
Immaculate Mary, meek and humble of heart,
conform our hearts to the Heart of Jesus.

Let us pray: O most merciful God, who for the salvation of sinners and the refuge of the wretched, has made the Immaculate Heart of Mary most like in tenderness and pity to the Heart of Jesus, grant that we, who now commemorate her most sweet and loving heart, may by her merits and intercession ever live in the fellowship of the hearts of both Mother and Son, through the same Christ our Lord. Amen.

Litany to Our Lady of Victory

Lord, have mercy on us.
Christ, have mercy on us.
Lord, have mercy on us.
Christ, hear us. Christ, graciously hear us.
God, the Father of Heaven, have mercy on us.
God, the Son, Redeemer of the world, have mercy on us.
God, the Holy Spirit, have mercy on us.
Holy Trinity, one God, have mercy on us.

Our Lady of Victory, pray for us.
Victorious Daughter of the Father, pray for us.
Victorious Mother of the Son, pray for us.
Victorious Spouse of the Holy Spirit, pray for us.
Victorious Servant of the Holy Trinity, pray for us.
Victorious in Your Immaculate Conception, pray for us.
Victorious in Crushing the Serpent's Head, pray for us.
Victorious over All the Children of Adam, pray for us.
Victorious over All Enemies, pray for us.
Victorious in Response to the Angel Gabriel, pray for us
Victorious in Your Wedding to St. Joseph, pray for us.
Victorious in the Birth of Christ, pray for us.
Victorious in the Flight into Egypt, pray for us.
Victorious in Your Exile, pray for us.
Victorious in Your Home at Nazareth, pray for us.
Victorious in Finding Christ in the Temple, pray for us.
Victorious in the Mission of Your Son, pray for us.
Victorious in His Passion and Death, pray for us.
Victorious in His Resurrection and Ascension, pray for us.
Victorious in the Coming of the Holy Spirit, pray for us.
Victorious in Your Sorrows and Joys, pray for us.
Victorious in Your Glorious Assumption, pray for us.
Victorious in Angels who Remained Faithful, pray for us.
Victorious in the Happiness of the Saints, pray for us.
Victorious in the Message of the Prophets, pray for us.
Victorious in the Testimony of the Patriarchs, pray for us.
Victorious in the Zeal of the Apostles, pray for us.
Victorious in the Witness of the Evangelists, pray for us.
Victorious in the Wisdom of the Doctors, pray for us.
Victorious in the Deeds of the Confessors, pray for us.
Victorious in the Triumph of All Holy Women, pray for us.
Victorious in the Faithfulness of the Martyrs, pray for us.

Victorious in Your Powerful Intercession, pray for us.
Victorious Under Your Many Titles, pray for us.
Victorious at the Moment of Death, pray for us.

Lamb of God, who takes away the sins of the world,
spare us, O Lord.
Lamb of God, who takes away the sins of the world,
hear us, O Lord.
Lamb of God, who takes away the sins of the world,
have mercy, O Lord.

Pray for us, Blessed Lady of Victory, that we may be made worthy of the promises of Christ.

Let us pray. Our Lady of Victory, we have unshaken confidence in your influence with your Son, our Lord Jesus Christ. Humbly we ask your intercession for all of us associated under your title, Our Lady of Victory. We beg your powerful assistance also for our own personal needs *(please mention those needs here)*.

In your maternal kindness, please ask Jesus to forgive all our sins and failings, and to secure His blessings for us and for all the works of charity dedicated to your name. We implore you to obtain for us the grace of sharing Christ's victory and yours forever in the life that knows no ending. May we join you there to praise forever the Father, His Son, Jesus Christ, and the Holy Spirit, one God, for all ages to come. Amen.

Litany to Mary of Nazareth

Glory to you, God our Creator.
Breathe into us new life, new meaning.
Glory to you, God our Creator.
Lead us into the way of peace and justice.
Glory to you, healing Spirit.
Transform us to empower others.

Mary, wellspring of peace, be our guide.
Model of strength, be our guide.
Model of gentleness, be our guide.
Model of trust, be our guide.
Model of patience, be our guide.
Model of courage, be our guide.

Model of risk, be our guide.
Model of openness, be our guide.
Model of perseverance, be our guide.

Oppressed woman, lead us to life.
Liberator of the oppressed, lead us to life.
Marginalized woman, lead us to life.
Comforter of the afflicted, lead us to life.
Cause of our joy, lead us to life.
Sign of contradiction, lead us to life.
Breaker of bondage, lead us to life.
Political refugee, lead us to life.

Mother of the liberator, pray for us.
Mother of the homeless, pray for us.
Mother of the dying, pray for us.
Mother of the nonviolent, pray for us.
Widowed mother, pray for us.
Mother of a political prisoner, pray for us.
Mother of the condemned, pray for us.
Mother of the executed criminal, pray for us.

Woman of mercy, empower us.
Woman of faith, empower us.
Woman of contemplation, empower us.
Woman of vision, empower us.
Woman of wisdom and understanding, empower us.
Woman of grace and truth, empower us.
Woman, pregnant with hope, empower us.
Woman, centered in God, empower us.
Seeker of sanctuary, empower us.
First disciple, empower us.
Sharer in Christ's ministry, empower us.
Participant in Christ's Passion, empower us.
Seeker of God's will, empower us.
Witness of Christ's Resurrection, empower us.

Let us pray: Mary, Queen of Peace, we entrust our lives to you. Shelter us from war, hatred, and oppression. Teach us to live in peace, to educate ourselves for peace. Inspire us to act justly, to reverence all God has made. Root peace firmly in our hearts and in our world. Amen.

Litany of Our Lady of Lourdes

Lord, have mercy. Lord, have mercy.
Christ, have mercy. Christ, have mercy.
Lord, have mercy. Lord, have mercy.
Christ, hear us. Christ, graciously hear us.
God the Father of Heaven, have mercy on us.
God the Son, Redeemer of the world, have mercy on us.
God the Holy Spirit, have mercy on us.
Holy Trinity, one God, have mercy on us.

Holy Mary, pray for us.
Holy Mother of God, pray for us.
Mother of Christ, pray for us.
Mother of our Savior, pray for us.

Our Lady of Lourdes, help of Christians, pray for us.
Our Lady of Lourdes, source of love, pray for us.
Our Lady of Lourdes, mother of the poor, pray for us.
Our Lady of Lourdes, mother of the handicapped, pray for us.
Our Lady of Lourdes, mother of orphans, pray for us.
Our Lady of Lourdes, mother of all children, pray for us.
Our Lady of Lourdes, mother of all nations, pray for us.
Our Lady of Lourdes, mother of the Church, pray for us.
Our Lady of Lourdes, friend of the lonely, pray for us.
Our Lady of Lourdes, comforter of those who mourn, pray for us.
Our Lady of Lourdes, shelter of the homeless, pray for us.
Our Lady of Lourdes, guide of travelers, pray for us.
Our Lady of Lourdes, strength of the weak, pray for us.
Our Lady of Lourdes, refuge of sinners. pray for us.
Our Lady of Lourdes, comforter of the suffering, pray for us.
Our Lady of Lourdes, help of the dying, pray for us.
Queen of heaven, pray for us.
Queen of peace, pray for us.
Lamb of God, you take away the sins of the world, spare us, O Lord.
Lamb of God, you take away the sins of the world, graciously hear us, O Lord.
Lamb of God, you take away the sins of the world, have mercy on us.

Let us pray: Grant us, your servants, we pray you, Lord God, to enjoy perpetual health of mind and body. By the glorious intercession of Blessed Mary, ever Virgin, may we be delivered from present sorrows and enjoy everlasting happiness, through Christ our Lord. Amen.

Litany of Our Lady of Seven Sorrows

Lord, have mercy on us.
Christ, have mercy on us.
Lord, have mercy on us.

Christ, hear us. Christ, graciously hear us.

God, the Father of heaven, have mercy on us.
God the Son, Redeemer of the world, have mercy on us.
God the Holy Spirit, have mercy on us.

Holy Mary, Mother of God, pray for us.
Holy Virgin of virgins, pray for us.
Mother of the Crucified, pray for us.
Sorrowful Mother, pray for us.
Mournful Mother, pray for us.
Sighing Mother, pray for us.
Afflicted Mother, pray for us.
Forsaken Mother, pray for us.
Desolate Mother, pray for us.
Mother most sad, pray for us.
Mother set around with anguish, pray for us.
Mother overwhelmed by grief, pray for us.
Mother transfixed by a sword, pray for us.
Mother crucified in thy heart, pray for us.
Mother bereaved of thy Son, pray for us.
Sighing Dove, pray for us.
Mother of Dolors, pray for us.
Fount of tears, pray for us.
Sea of bitterness, pray for us.
Field of tribulation, pray for us.
Mass of suffering, pray for us.
Mirror of patience, pray for us.
Rock of constancy, pray for us.
Remedy in perplexity, pray for us.
Joy of the afflicted, pray for us.
Ark of the desolate, pray for us.

Refuge of the abandoned, pray for us.
Shield of the oppressed, pray for us.
Conqueror of the incredulous, pray for us.
Solace of the wretched, pray for us.
Medicine of the sick, pray for us.
Help of the faint, pray for us.
Strength of the weak, pray for us.
Protectress of those who fight, pray for us.
Haven of the shipwrecked, pray for us.
Calmer of tempests, pray for us.
Companion of the sorrowful, pray for us.
Retreat of those who groan, pray for us.
Terror of the treacherous, pray for us.
Standard-bearer of the martyrs, pray for us.
Treasure of the faithful, pray for us.
Light of confessors, pray for us.
Pearl of virgins, pray for us.
Comfort of widows, pray for us.
Joy of all saints, pray for us.
Queen of thy servants, pray for us.
Holy Mary, who alone art unexampled, pray for us.

Pray for us, most Sorrowful Virgin, that we may be made worthy of the promises of Christ.
Let us pray: O God, in whose Passion, according to the prophecy of Simeon, a sword of grief pierced through the most sweet soul of Thy glorious Blessed Virgin Mother Mary, grant that we, who celebrate the memory of her Seven Sorrows, may obtain the happy effect of Thy Passion, Who lives and reigns world without end. Amen.

Litany of the Life of Mary

Lord, have mercy.
Christ, have mercy.
Lord, have mercy.

God the Father of Heaven, have mercy on us.
God the Son, Redeemer of the world, have mercy on us.
God the Holy Spirit, dwelling in the souls of the just,
have mercy on us.

Holy Mary, pray for us.
Holy Virgin, sprung from the race of David, pray for us.

Holy Virgin, of the root of Jesse, pray for us.
Holy Virgin, conceived without Original Sin, pray for us.
Holy Virgin, presented in childhood in the temple, pray for us.
Holy Virgin, espoused to the just Joseph, pray for us.
Holy Virgin, bound by an inviolable vow of chastity, pray for us.
Holy Virgin, gloriously saluted by the Angel, pray for us.
Holy Virgin, full of grace, pray for us.
Holy Virgin, blessed among all women, pray for us.
Holy Virgin, consenting to the plea of Heaven, pray for us.
Holy Virgin, conceiving by the operation of the Holy Spirit, pray for us.
Holy Virgin, bearing in thy womb the God-Man, pray for us.
Holy Virgin, Mother of the Lord, pray for us.
Holy Virgin, Mother of the true Solomon, pray for us.
Holy Virgin, Mother of God, pray for us.
Holy Virgin, visiting thy cousin Elizabeth, pray for us.
Holy Virgin, blest land whence sprung the Savior, pray for us.
Holy Virgin, holy gate through which the King of Heaven alone may pass, pray for us.
Holy Virgin, journeying to Bethlehem with thy spouse Joseph, pray for us.
Holy Virgin, bringing into the world thy Divine Son, pray for us.
Holy Virgin, Mother of thine own Creator, pray for us.
Holy Virgin, laying God the Son in a manger, pray for us.
Holy Virgin, visited by the shepherds, pray for us.
Holy Virgin, saluted by the Magi, pray for us.
Holy Virgin, presenting thy Son to be circumcised, pray for us.
Holy Virgin, submitting to the law of purification, pray for us.
Holy Virgin, offering thy dear Son in the temple, pray for us.
Holy Virgin, flying into Egypt to save thy Child, pray for us.
Holy Virgin, returning into the land of Israel, pray for us.
Holy Virgin, leading an obscure life at Nazareth, pray for us.

Holy Virgin, keeping the feasts prescribed by the law, pray for us.

Holy Virgin, afflicted at the loss of thy Child when He was twelve years old, pray for us.

Holy Virgin, sorrowfully seeking thy Child for three days, pray for us.

Holy Virgin, honoring with thy presence the marriage feast of Cana, pray for us.

Holy Virgin, graciously representing to thy Son the want of wine, pray for us.

Holy Virgin, obtaining Christ's first public miracle by thy intercession, pray for us.

Holy Virgin, following thy Son in His ministrations, pray for us.

Holy Virgin, sharing the sorrows of thy Son, pray for us.

Holy Virgin, standing at the foot of the Cross, pray for us.

Holy Virgin, confided by thy Son to John the Beloved Disciple, pray for us.

Holy Virgin, pierced with a sword of sorrow, pray for us.

Holy Virgin, filled with the Holy Spirit on the day of Pentecost, pray for us.

Holy Virgin, assumed by thy Son into Heaven, pray for us.

Holy Virgin, reigning in Heaven, our Queen, pray for us.

Holy Virgin, called Blessed by all generations, pray for us.

Lamb of God, who takes away the sins of the world, spare us, O Lord.

Lamb of God, who takes away the sins of the world, graciously hear us, O Lord.

Lamb of God, who takes away the sins of the world, have mercy on us.

Pray for us, O Holy Mother of God, that we may be made worthy of the promises of Christ.

Let us pray: Protect, O Lord, Thy servants by Thy gracious and abundant help, and grant that our confidence in the protection of Blessed Mary ever Virgin, and our humble imitation of her holy life, may obtain for us security against all enemies and all dangers, through our Lord Jesus Christ. Amen.

Litany to Mary, Mother of Life

Lord, have mercy. Lord, have mercy.
Christ, have mercy. Christ, have mercy.
Lord, have mercy. Lord, have mercy.

God our Father in Heaven, have mercy on us.
God the Son, Redeemer of the world, have mercy on us.
God the Holy Spirit, have mercy on us.

Holy Mary, pray for us.
Holy Mother of God, pray for us.
Most honored of virgins, pray for us.
Mother of Christ, pray for us.
Mother of the Church, pray for us.
Mother of divine grace, pray for us.
Mother most pure, pray for us.
Mother of chaste love, pray for us.
Mother and virgin, pray for us.
Sinless mother, pray for us.
Dearest of mothers, pray for us.
Model of motherhood, pray for us.
Mother of good counsel, pray for us.
Mother of our Creator, pray for us.

Virgin most wise, pray for us.
Virgin rightly praised, pray for us.
Virgin rightly renowned, pray for us.
Virgin most powerful, pray for us.
Virgin gentle in mercy, pray for us.
Faithful virgin, pray for us.
Mirror of justice, pray for us.
Throne of wisdom, pray for us.
Cause of our joy, pray for us.
Shrine of the Spirit, pray for us.
Glory of Israel, pray for us.
Vessel of selfless devotion, pray for us.
Mystical Rose, pray for us.
Tower of David, pray for us.
Tower of ivory, pray for us.
House of gold, pray for us.
Ark of the Covenant, pray for us.
Gate of Heaven, pray for us.
Morning Star, pray for us.

Health of the sick, pray for us.
Refuge of sinners, pray for us.
Comfort of the troubled, pray for us.
Help of Christians, pray for us.

Queen of angels, pray for us.
Queen of patriarchs and prophets, pray for us.
Queen of Apostles and martyrs, pray for us.
Queen of confessors and virgins, pray for us.
Queen conceived without Original Sin, pray for us.
Queen assumed into Heaven, pray for us.
Queen of the rosary, pray for us.
Queen of families, pray for us.
Queen of peace, pray for us.

Lamb of God, you take away the sins of the world,
pray for us, holy Mother of God.
Lamb of God, you take away the sins of the world,
pray for us, holy Mother of God.
Lamb of God, you take away the sins of the world,
pray for us, holy Mother of God.

Let us pray: Loving God, You are our Creator and benevolent giver of life, give to your people health in mind and body. Through the intercession of the Virgin Mary, free us from the sorrows of this life and lead us to happiness in the life to come. Grant this through our Lord, Jesus Christ, who lives and reigns with you, one God, for ever and ever. Amen.

Novena to Our Lady of Good Remedy

O Queen of Heaven and earth, most holy Virgin, we venerate you. You are the beloved daughter of the Most High God, the chosen mother of the Incarnate Word, the immaculate spouse of the Holy Spirit, the sacred vessel of the Most Holy Trinity.

O mother of the Divine Redeemer, who under the title of Our Lady of Good Remedy comes to the aid of all who call upon you, extend your maternal protection to us. We depend on you, dear Mother, as helpless and needy children depend on a tender and loving mother.

Hail, Mary ...

O Lady of Good Remedy, source of unfailing help, grant that we may draw from your treasury of graces in our time of need.

Touch the hearts of sinners, that they may seek reconciliation and forgiveness. Bring comfort to the afflicted and the lonely; help the poor and the hopeless; aid the sick and the suffering. May they be healed in body and strengthened in spirit to endure their sufferings with patient resignation and Christian fortitude.

Hail, Mary …

Dear Lady of Good Remedy, source of unfailing help, your compassionate heart knows a remedy for every affliction and misery we encounter in this life. Help me with your prayers and intercession to find a remedy for my problems and needs, especially for *(mention your special intentions here)*.

On my part, O loving Mother, I pledge myself to a more intensely Christian lifestyle, to a more careful observance of the laws of God, to be more conscientious in fulfilling the obligations of my state in life, and to strive to be a source of healing in this broken world of ours.

Dear Lady of Good Remedy, be ever present to me, and through your intercession, may I enjoy health of body and peace of mind, and grow stronger in the faith and in the love of your Son, Jesus.

Hail, Mary …

Pray for us, O Holy Mother of Good Remedy, that we may deepen our dedication to your Son and make the world alive with His Spirit. Amen.

The Memorare

Remember, O most gracious Virgin Mary, that never was it known that anyone who fled to your protection, implored your help, or sought your intercession was left unaided. Inspired by this confidence, I fly unto you, O Virgin of virgins, my Mother. To you do I come, before you I stand, sinful and sorrowful. O Mother of the Word Incarnate, despise not my petitions, but in your mercy hear and answer me. Amen.

CATHOLIC PRAYERS

Sign of the Cross

In the name of the Father,
and of the Son,
and of the Holy Spirit.
Amen.

In nomine Patris
et Filii,
et Spiritus Sancti.
Amen.

The Lord's Prayer

Our Father, who art in heaven,
hallowed be thy name;
thy kingdom come,
thy will be done on earth
as it is in heaven.
Give us this day our daily
bread, and forgive us our
trespasses as we forgive those
who trespass against us,
and lead us not into temptation,
but deliver us from evil.
Amen.

Pater noster, qui es in caelis,
sanctificetur nomen tuum;
adveniat regnum tuum;
fiat voluntas tua
sicut in caelo, et in terra.
Panem nostrum quotidianum
da nobis hodie,
et dimitte nobis debita nostra,
sicut et nos dimittimus
debitoribus nostris et ne nos
inducas in tentationem
sed libera nos a malo.
Amen.

The Hail Mary

Hail Mary, full of grace,
the Lord is with thee.
Blessed art thou among
women, and blessed is the
fruit of thy womb, Jesus.
Holy Mary, Mother of God,
pray for us sinners now and
at the hour of our death.
Amen.

Ave, Maria, gratia plena,
Dominus tecum.
Benedicta tu in mulieribus
et benedictus fructus
ventris tui, Iesus.
Sancta Maria, Mater Dei,
ora pro nobis peccatoribus,
nunc et in hora mortis nostrae.
Amen.

Glory Be to the Father

Glory be to the Father,
and to the Son,
and to the Holy Spirit.
As it was in the beginning,
is now, and ever shall be,
world without end. Amen.

Gloria Patri, et Filio,
et Spiritui Sancto.
Sicut erat in principio,
et nunc, et semper,
et in saecula saeculorum.
Amen.

Hail, Holy Queen

Hail, Holy Queen, Mother of Mercy, our life, our sweetness, and our hope. To thee do we cry, poor banished children of Eve. To thee do we send up our sighs, mourning and weeping in this valley of tears. Turn then, most gracious advocate, thine eyes of mercy toward us, and after this our exile, show unto us the blessed fruit of thy womb, Jesus.
O clement, O loving,
O sweet Virgin Mary,
pray for us, O holy Mother of God, that we may be made worthy of the promises of Christ.
Amen.

Salve, Regina, mater-misericordiae, vita, dulcedo et spes nostra, salve. Ad te clamamus, exsules filii Evae. Ad te suspiramus gementes et flentes in hac lacrimarum valle. Eia ergo, advocata nostra, illos tuos misericordes oculos ad nos converte et Iesum, benedictum fructum ventris tui, nobis post hoc exsilium ostende.
O clemens, O pia, O dulcis Virgo Maria!
Ora pro nobis,
sancta Dei Genetrix.
Ut digni efficiamur promissionibus Christi.
Amen.

The Apostles' Creed

I believe in God,
the Father almighty,
Creator of heaven and earth.
I believe in Jesus Christ,
his only Son, our Lord.
He was conceived by the power of the Holy Spirit,
born of the Virgin Mary,
suffered under Pontius Pilate,
was crucified, died, and was buried. He descended into hell. On the third day he rose again. He ascended into heaven and is seated at the right hand of the Father. He will come again to judge the living and the dead. I believe in the Holy Spirit, the holy catholic church, the communion of saints, the forgiveness of sins, the resurrection of the body, and life everlasting. Amen.

Credo in Deum, Patrem omnipotentem, Creatorem caeli et terrae; et in Iesum Christum, Filium eius unicum, Dominum nostrum, qui conceptus est de Spiritu Sancto, natus ex Maria Virgine, passus sub Pontio Pilato, crucifixus, mortuus, et sepultus. Descendit ad inferos; tertia die resurrexit a mortuis, ascendit ad caelos, sedet ad dexteram Dei, Patris omnipotentis in de venturus est judicare vivos et mortuos. Credo in Spiritum Sanctum, sanctam ecclesiam catholicam, sanctorum communionem, remissionem peccatorum, carnis resurrexionem, vitam aeternam.
Amen.

The Mysteries of the Rosary

The Joyful Mysteries (Monday and Saturday)
The Annunciation by the Angel to Mary
The Visitation of Mary to Elizabeth
The Birth of Our Lord in Bethlehem
The Presentation of Jesus in the Temple
The Finding of the Child Jesus in the Temple

The Luminous Mysteries (Thursday)
The Baptism of Jesus in the Jordan
The Miracle of the Wine at Cana
The Proclamation of the Kingdom
The Transfiguration of Jesus
The Institution of the Eucharist

The Sorrowful Mysteries (Tuesday and Friday)
The Agony in the Garden
The Scourging at the Pillar
The Crowning with Thorns
The Carrying of the Cross
The Crucifixion and Death of Our Lord

The Glorious Mysteries (Sunday and Wednesday)
The Resurrection of Jesus from the Dead
The Ascension of Jesus into Heaven
The Descent of the Holy Spirit on the Apostles
The Assumption of Mary into Heaven
The Crowning of Mary as Queen of Heaven and Earth

How to Pray the Rosary

Make the Sign of the Cross and, while holding the crucifix, say the Apostles' Creed. On the first bead, say an Our Father, Hail Marys on the next three beads, and a Glory Be on the last bead. For each of the five decades on the main part of the rosary, announce the mystery, say an Our Father and then ten Hail Marys while fingering each bead and meditating on the mystery.

Finish each decade with a Glory Be and the prayer requested by Our Lady of Fatima ("O my Jesus, forgive us our sins, save us from the fire of hell, lead all souls to heaven, especially those in most need of your mercy.").

After the five decades, say the Hail Holy Queen and, before making the Sign of the Cross, say: "O God, whose only begotten Son, by His life, Death, and Resurrection, has purchased for us the rewards of eternal life, grant, we beseech Thee, that by meditating on these mysteries of the most holy rosary of the Blessed Virgin Mary, we may imitate what they contain and obtain what they promise, through the same Christ our Lord. Amen."

Stations of the Cross

While standing before each station, say while genuflecting, "We adore you, O Christ, and we praise you, because by your holy Cross you have redeemed the world." Then say an Our Father, a Hail Mary, and a Glory Be to the Father while meditating on the particular event during the Passion and Death of our Lord.

First Station:	Jesus is condemned to death by Pontius Pilate.
Second Station:	Jesus carries His Cross.
Third Station:	Jesus falls the first time.
Fourth Station:	Jesus meets His sorrowful mother.
Fifth Station:	Simon of Cyrene helps Jesus to carry His Cross.
Sixth Station:	Veronica wipes the face of Jesus.
Seventh Station:	Jesus falls the second time.
Eighth Station:	Jesus meets the women of Jerusalem.
Ninth Station:	Jesus falls a third time.
Tenth Station:	Jesus is stripped of His clothes.
Eleventh Station:	Jesus is nailed to the Cross.
Twelfth Station:	Jesus dies on the Cross.
Thirteenth Station:	Jesus is taken down from the Cross.
Fourteenth Station:	The body of Jesus is laid in the tomb.

Act of Contrition *(Traditional Version)*

O my God, I am heartily sorry for having offended Thee, and I detest all my sins because I dread the loss of heaven and the pains of hell, but most of all because they have offended Thee, my God, who art all good and deserving of all my love. I firmly resolve, with the help of thy grace, to confess my sins, to do penance, and to amend my life. Amen.

Act of Contrition *(Alternate Version)*

O my God, I am sorry for my sins with all my heart. In choosing to do wrong and failing to do good, I have sinned against You whom I should love above all things. I firmly intend, with your help, to do penance, to sin no more, and to avoid whatever leads me to sin. Amen.

Act of Contrition *(Alternate Version)*

Lord Jesus, Son of God, have mercy on me, a sinner.

Prayer for the Church

O God, our refuge and our strength, look down in mercy on your people who cry to You, and by the intercession of the glorious and Immaculate Virgin Mary, Mother of God, of St. Joseph her spouse, of your blessed Apostles Peter and Paul, and of all the saints, in your mercy and goodness hear the prayers that we pour forth for the conversion of sinners and for the freedom and exaltation of our Holy Mother the Church, through the same Christ our Lord. Amen.

Prayer to St. Michael

St. Michael, the Archangel, defend us in the battle. Be our protection against the wickedness and snares of the Devil. May God rebuke him, we humbly pray, and do you, O Prince of the Heavenly Host, by the power of God cast into Hell Satan and all the evil spirits who wander through the world seeking the ruin of souls. Amen.

The Divine Praises

Blessed be God.
Blessed be His Holy Name.
Blessed be Jesus Christ, true God and true Man.
Blessed be the Name of Jesus.
Blessed be His most Sacred Heart.
Blessed be His most Precious Blood.
Blessed be Jesus in the most Holy Sacrament of the Altar.
Blessed be the Holy Spirit, the Paraclete.
Blessed be the great Mother of God, Mary most holy.
Blessed be her holy and Immaculate Conception.
Blessed be her glorious Assumption.
Blessed be the name of Mary, Virgin and Mother.
Blessed be St. Joseph, her most chaste spouse.
Blessed be God in His angels and in His saints.

A. Stankard
Mary is praying for you

BIBLIOGRAPHY

Apostoli, Fr. Andrew, CFR. *Fatima for Today*
A Woman Clothed With the Sun. Edited by John J. Delaney

Benedict XVI, Pope. *Jesus of Nazareth*
Bertone, Tarcisius Cardinal. *The Last Secret of Fatima*

Catechism of the Catholic Church
Cranston, Ruth. *The Miracle of Lourdes*

De Montfort, St. Louis Mary. *The Secret of the Rosary*
Does the Bible Support Catholic Beliefs? Edited by David Lang
Drummey, James J. *Catholic Replies*
__________. *Catholic Replies 2*
__________. *"Who Do You Say That I Am?"*
__________. and Msgr. Paul J. Hayes. *Catholicism & Scripture*

Encyclopedia of Catholic Devotions and Practices.
Edited by Ann Ball

Groeschel, Fr. Benedict J., C.F.R. *A Still, Small Voice*

Ilibagiza, Immaculee. *Our Lady of Kibeho*

John Paul II, Pope. *Guardian of the Redeemer*
__________. *Mother of the Redeemer*
__________. *Rosary of the Virgin Mary*

Keating, Karl. *Catholicism and Fundamentalism*

Magnificat. *The Wonders of Lourdes*

Ricciotti, Giuseppe. *The Life of Christ*

Sheed, Frank. *To Know Christ Jesus*
Sheen, Fulton J. *Life of Christ*

Vatican Council II. Dogmatic Constitution on the Church
(Lumen Gentium)

INDEX